MW00811214

Doing Business in Germany

Doing Business in Germany

A Concise Guide to Understanding Germans and their Business Practices

Andra Riemhofer

Doing Business in Germany: A Concise Guide to Understanding Germans and their Business Practices

Copyright © Business Expert Press, LLC, 2019.

All rights reserved. No part of this publication may be reproduced, stored in a retrieval system, or transmitted in any form or by any means—electronic, mechanical, photocopy, recording, or any other except for brief quotations, not to exceed 400 words, without the prior permission of the publisher.

First published in 2019 by
Business Expert Press, LLC
222 East 46th Street, New York, NY 10017
www.businessexpertpress.com

ISBN-13: 978-1-94819-884-4 (paperback)
ISBN-13: 978-1-94819-885-1 (e-book)

Business Expert Press International Business Collection

Collection ISSN: 1948-2752 (print)
Collection ISSN: 1948-2760 (electronic)

Cover and interior design by Exeter Premedia Services Private Ltd., Chennai, India

First edition: 2019

10 9 8 7 6 5 4 3 2 1

Printed in the United States of America.

For my dear friend, Ines, whom I most likely would not have met had there still been two Germanys.

Abstract

Germany is the strongest economy in Europe, and one of the largest worldwide. The business climate is good, people are highly skilled, and consumers have plenty of spending money in their pockets; for companies that are doing business internationally, Germany is a market that simply cannot be overlooked.

However, many business relationships with Germans come to an end even before they begin; intercultural differences very often result in misunderstandings, frustration, and an unnecessary loss of time and money. Especially with Germans, even small things can be crucial when you are speaking to a (potential) business contact.

This book aims at helping students and professionals avoid the common pitfalls that international business people typically step into when dealing with Germans for the very first time. Unlike with the other business- or textbooks focusing on culture, this book will do more than just arm you with some simple "Dos and Don'ts;" it will provide interesting and easy-to-understand descriptions and anecdotes that highlight the cultural standards and dimensions that are (typically) theoretically discussed in scientific texts. Essentially, while talking about what makes "the average" German tick, readers will be equipped with the relevant background knowledge. The focus of the book is to help readers understand how certain concepts and values influence the way Germans like to do business. It will guide them on how to successfully interact with Germans, whether at trade shows, during virtual and face-to-face meetings, or when they are negotiating their first contract.

Keywords

Germany; Business Culture; International Marketing; Business Etiquette; Business Development; Trade Shows; Made in Germany; Dual Vocational Education and Training (Duale Berufsausbildung); Mittelstand; Hidden Champions; Cross-cultural Management

Contents

List of Figure and Tables

Preface

Germany is currently in a foul mood. Foreigners might argue that we always are, but now, even *I* notice. I am observing a decisive rift in our society, and while I intend to brief you on what makes the "typical German" tick, the nation, or more precisely those dominating the public discourse, seem to be suffering from a full-fledged identity crisis. What is going on in my home country these days goes beyond the common practice of soul-searching and collective navel-gazing, and woe betide anyone who does not have a clear opinion on the matter! Ambiguity tolerance is, for sure, not a German virtue (Şenocak 2011, p. 98), and maybe that is a good starting point to discuss what, respectively who, is German.

There are voices of third-generation immigrants who are tired of having to articulate whether they would identify themselves as German(s) or Turks, for example; ever since politicians, talk shows, and comedians have zeroed in on the Turkish President Recep Tayyip Erdoğan as the antithesis of an enlightened Europe, some of those whose grandparents came to Germany as so-called "Gastarbeiter" (guest workers) during the "Wirtschaftswunder" (economic miracle) in the 1960s have been voicing their frustration about the subtle or open discrimination they, as individuals or a group, have been facing throughout their lives. They let off steam on YouTube, etcetera, and the echo is loud and nasty; not exactly civilized, well-mannered, or—one could also say—cultured.

Is it high time we define some behavior rules and write them down? Germans are fond of rules and are very much in favor of putting things in writing. Former Interior Minister Thomas de Maizière wasn't the first and will not be the last to publicly argue in favor of a catalog of dos and don'ts labeled "Deutsche Leitkultur" (German guiding or leading culture), something those living in Germany, according to his world view, shall identify with. "We are an open society. We show our face. We are not burka!," he wrote in a guest editorial for the popular (one could also say populist) Sunday newspaper *Bild am Sonntag* in April 2017 (Huggler 2017). De Maizière argued that there was an indigenous dominant culture in Germany that should be protected. By compelling people to shake hands? Seriously? I cannot help but conclude that his remarks were rather to entrench inequalities and marginalize many of those who just recently arrived in Germany from an eastern or southern direction. "There is something beyond our language, constitution, and respect for fundamental rights that binds us in our hearts, that makes us different, and distinguishes us from others," he wrote (ibid.).

Only one year later, in early 2018, the freshly appointed Bavarian Minister President Markus Söder managed to make his point about the worthiness of (or the need for) the protection of Western Christian civilization (while being ridiculed by many people in and outside his dominion), enforcing that "'als sichtbares Bekenntnis zu den Grundwerten der Rechts- und Gesellschaftsordnung in Bayern und Deutschland'" (ZEIT ONLINE 2018) (as a visible commitment to the fundamental values of the legal and social order in Bavaria and Germany), a cross shall be visibly hung at the entrance of every public building in the state (there are 16 federal states in Germany; Bavaria is in the south and commonly known for BMW and the Oktoberfest). The local head of the Catholic Church, Archbishop of Munich and Freising, Cardinal Marx, condemned this interpretation (one could also say hijacking) of the symbol (Drobinski and Wetzel 2018). What is going on, and where did all this come from?

When I ask people in Germany what years they vividly remember, then, according to their age, or depending on how long they have lived in Germany, almost all of them mention 1989, when the wall came down, followed by the reunification of East and West Germany in 1990. Many also fondly recall 2006, when Germany hosted the FIFA World Cup and when, after a long period of national self-denial, for the very first time, people confidently hoisted the German flag. That had, at least in a non-official context, been quite a taboo after the Nazi regime and Second World War. The official slogan "Die Welt zu Gast bei Freunden" (literally: the world as a guest with friends, or maybe more precisely: the world is hosted by friends) was translated for the English-speaking world as "A time to make friends." I remember those four weeks as an ongoing party during which Germans painted their faces in the national colors black, red, and gold, with many of them wearing matching wigs, plastic flower-chains, goggles, t-shirts, and we do not need to know what else (most probably white socks), and embraced whoever happened to be within arm's reach whenever the German national team scored. Which must have happened quite a lot considering that we (notice the "*we*"!) managed—to at least—win third place. But let's not talk about the (lost) World Cup; rather, let me indulge in reminiscences of that German "Sommermärchen" (Summer Fairy Tale), in which a long-divided people were quite unbiasedly celebrating their national identity. That was a new thing! A phenomenon that was also observed with growing anguish from some peripheries of society.

Maybe this newfound spirit of unity helped (many) people cope with the impacts of the world financial crises of 2008 triggered by the bankruptcy of the U.S. investment bank Lehman Brothers that severely affected the (current) world export champion Germany only two years later. Companies were doing their utmost not to lay-off their skilled labor force. Shorter hours at reduced wages were the reality for many workers and employees for many months. Some companies used the "free time" for trainings to upskill their workforce. The government invested in expanding the transport infrastructure, granted tax reductions, and launched a program called "Abwrackprämie" to make people buy new cars even though the economy was down; if you sacrificed your still-good-enough-but-slightly-outdated vehicle to the scrap metal press, your new car was subsidized by 2,500 euros from specially allocated government funds. The economy slowly picked up speed and the former "sick man of Europe" quickly became the class winner of the European Union. The success came at a price though, and I am not talking about how our popularity suffered when the former German Minister of Finance, Wolfgang Schäuble, insisted on introducing severe cost-cutting programs to be implemented by some of our less fortunate European neighbors.

One major reason for Germany's success was the flexibilization of the labor market, already in progress, although it had the undesirable side-effect of shoving more and more people into precarious working and living conditions. Along with the so-called *Hartz IV* reforms (2005), which meant steep cuts, especially for the long-term unemployed, many nowadays see the highly held principle of a social market economy, *Soziale Marktwirtschaft*, go down the drain. Also known as *Rhine Capitalism*, the Adenauer administration after the Second World War had introduced an economic principle that was meant to combine a free market capitalist economic system with social policies. Starting with the baby boomer generation, people born and brought up in (West) Germany were raised to believe in the superiority of a fair competition welfare state. Until a few years ago, there was no need for low-paid workers to accept two or three jobs to make ends meet, and if you were given notice (dismissal protection has always made this difficult for employers in Germany), a densely woven net of social security was there to rescue you. Looking at these instruments of social policy, what is currently offered might not be exactly what many people from the former German Democratic Republic would have hoped for when they lost their jobs during the reunification process—often overnight. In the eastern parts of the now united Germany, the State had taken care of full employment, even when it was not exactly cultivating an environment of highly productive working conditions. A growing number of people nowadays feel left behind, and ever since Chancellor Merkel in August 2015 (this is yet another year to remember) opened the borders to hundreds of thousands of refugees and said to the people "Wir schaffen das" (we can do it), the country seems to be divided into more than just two camps.

How is all this going to affect you as an international business person?

Firstly, if you think of Germany as a rather rich nation (ready to buy your products), be aware that, while the economy prospers, the gap between the rich and poor has been widening remarkably over the past few decades. I am going to dig deeper into matters of population, economy, spending power, and regional differences in Chapter 1 (where to locate Germany on the world map) and Chapter 3 (economy).

Secondly, depending on where you are coming from, how closely you follow the news on Germany in your home country, and perhaps in accordance with the perspectives offered by the news channels you follow, you might feel slightly uncertain about the kinds of people you are going to deal with. When you come to Germany to meet your business contacts or clients, you might talk to some of the many men and women who embrace diversity and multiculturalism and subscribe to the idea of an open society, very often, even volunteering to help refugees learn German, find their way through the jungle of German bureaucracy, or find a place to live when they are finally granted a permit of residence. And, you should not assume that these are solely retired people with plenty of time at their disposal! You might also meet people with a rather liberal state of mind, but who would argue that the current influx of immigrants is just too high for our society (how that society is defined, and who belongs to it, is under review) to handle. You might feel tension in these discussions and a perceived need for them to take a stand. You could be surprised to meet children of former immigrant generations who are clearly trying to distance themselves from the people who are currently seeking asylum because, for them, the current issues mean that their own cultural heritages and identities are (yet again) a topic of public concern. And, even if you were not to talk to some of those who find themselves represented by conservative and right-wing parties and organizations, you will most probably hear a lot about "culture," and what makes "the German" German. And, this is the kind of discourse I do *not* want to contribute to.

Rather, I intend to help you understand what makes people in Germany tick (Chapter 4), and explain how the past has shaped their minds (Chapter 2). Please do not skip these chapters because, only if you have understood certain concepts, values, and ideas presented therein, you will be able to better understand what I outline in the following chapters.

In Chapter 5, I will explain in more general terms how to fruitfully communicate with Germans and what pitfalls could lie before you that are best avoided. In Chapter 6, I will introduce typical business encounters such as attending trade shows, delivering presentations, and negotiating with Germans, and—using many examples—I will equip you with hands-on advice that you can use to develop strategies that will make you (even more) successful.

The book closes with some helpful tips on how to maintain (cordial) business relationships with your German business partners (Chapter 7).

A few words on the perspective from which the book is written. It is somewhat average in terms of who you most likely (statistically) would be dealing with: I was born in the 1970s, and after completing school at the age of 18 years, I first opted for a Duale Berufsausbildung (Dual Vocational Education and Training), becoming a Management Assistant in Publishing. A few years later, I studied business administration, and this is when I, for the first time, went abroad and had the opportunity to realize that what people in Germany (or at least members of the mainstream society) consider as "normal" does not apply everywhere else, at least not in India. I *did* survive the culture shock, and the interest in digging deeper into the topic of (inter-)cultural differences eventually led me to enroll in a master's program in Intercultural Communications and Cooperation a few years later. I am now assisting foreign (i.e., non-German) companies in developing business in Germany and help them avoid or overcome the pitfalls one typically could or would fall into when dealing with Germans for the very first time.

Acknowledgments

Thank you, Roystan La'Porte for considering me as an author for Business Expert Press and introducing me to the publisher. Thank you, Rachel George for being part of yet another writing project of mine. Your help in best possibly expressing my thoughts in English is very much appreciated. Thank you, Manoj Barve, Katharina Bömers, Achim Borse, Peter Burdyl, Cal O Cal, Sue De'Ath, Wiebke Drescher, Rena Dumont, Leslie Fleck, Osman Bayazit Genc, Andreas Hauser, Claudia Hefter, Gudrun Höhne, Daniel Ittstein, Stephan Janouch, Florian Käsbauer, Katharina Klaß and her language students (from Afghanistan, Eritrea, Greece, Iran, Nigeria, Pakistan, Somalia, Syria, and Yemen), Prajakta Kotasthane, Andrew MacKichan, Tina Oreskovich, Sven Riemann, Nigel Ruddock, Lukas Schmitz, Arjun Sachdev, Kuldeep Saraswat, Gustav Seehusen, Stewart Siegel, Bhupinder Singh, Hasan Syed, Abhilash V R, Manuel Vermeer, Petra Wagner, Alexander Wurz, David Zach, and many more people who decided to keep to the side lines, for offering your perspectives on the topic or reviewing parts of the text. I am also grateful to the participants of the seminars for academic job seekers on intercultural competence which I had been conducting this summer; the questions and resulting discussions with young professionals and seasoned executives who have often studied abroad, worked internationally, or have only recently come to Germany have greatly inspired many parts of this text.

Munich, October 2018

CHAPTER 1

Where to Locate Germany on the (Economic) World Map

Geography and Population

Even if you are not planning to *instantly* visit the country, knowing a few geographical coordinates might be useful. Germany is located in Central Europe and, with 357,168 square kilometers or 137,847 square miles, is one of the larger countries in the region. However, if you compare it with the size of the United States, for example, it might appear to you as rather small. Germany is about 85 percent the size of California (423,970 square kilometers), a little smaller than Japan, and approximately 1.5 times the size of Great Britain (Traveler's Digest 2014). If you are interested, you can use http://mapfrappe.com to compare Germany's dimensions with the country or state you live in.

Germany's biggest aviation hub is Frankfurt am Main (FRA), which is located in Germany's fifth largest city (approximately 750,000 inhabitants). If you fly in from São Paulo or Tokyo, the journey will take you about 12 hours; 11 hours, if you board an aircraft in Beijing or Johannesburg; and eight hours, if you fly out from New York or Mumbai. Coming from Dubai, you would disembark after a seven-hour flight. Moscow is as close as 3.5 hours. The German financial metropolis is situated somewhat in the center of the country and should not be confused with Frankfurt an der Oder, which is in the east of Germany, closer to Berlin and bordering Poland. Berlin is the nation's capital and, with about 3.7 million inhabitants, is the largest city in the country. Altogether, about 83 million people currently live in Germany (also refer to *Table 1.1: Key figures on population* [Federal Statistical Office n.d.]).

Table 1.1 Key figures on population

Population (March 31, 2018)	2018	82.8 mn
Foreign	2017	10.6 mn
With migrant background	2017	19.3 mn
Deaths	2017	784,901
Age of mother at first birth	2016	29.6
Total fertility rate (children per woman)	2016	1.59
Deaths	2017	932,272
Average age	2015	44
Average age at death		78
Men	2016	75
Women	2016	82
Net migration	2017	416,080
Households	2018	41.3 mn
Lone parents	2016	1.6 mn
Marriages	2017	407,466
Divorces	2017	153,501

A train ride from the second largest city Hamburg, in the north (approximately 1.8 million people), to Munich, in the south (about 1.5 million inhabitants), takes six hours. It covers about 600 kilometers (km) as the crow flies, and that is pretty much the greatest distance I can imagine you would likely travel in one day as a business person. In case you are used to measuring distances in miles (mi), just remember that with the metric system commonly used in most parts of the world, the prefix "kilo" means 1,000 times larger; in this case, larger than meters: 1 mi is about 1,609 meters, which is 1.6 km.

A journey from the sleepy provincial town of Flensburg (12 meters above the sea level), at the Danish border in the north (refer to the map displayed in Figure 1.1), to the picturesque tourist destination of Garmisch-Partenkirchen, at the foot of Germany's highest mountain Zugspitze (2,962 m or 9,718 ft) in the very south of Germany, is the longest distance I can think of to travel (about 1,000 km are to be covered in about nine hours, if you go by car). Most Germans would only be aware of the existence of Flensburg because that is where the Federal Motor Transport Authority (Kraftfahrt Bundesamt (KBA)) is located. In Germany,

Figure 1.1 Map of Germany

you get points for reckless driving; not brownie points, as you might suspect looking at how Germans often consider speeding a trivial offense, but malus points, which can cost you your driver's license. Yes, on the freeway (Autobahn), you can basically go as fast as your Volkswagen or Porsche might allow, but there *are* still defined speed limits that Germans often fail to notice (Kraftfahrt-Bundesamt n.d.), which is a paradox, considering how we are generally happy to strictly follow just about any rule.

Overall, I would say that traffic movement in Germany is quite calm, steady, and organized. Germans do not have the habit of taking U-turns in the middle of a crossroad (or only if nobody is looking), and if asked whether they, at a traffic bottleneck, for example, would prefer alternately merging traffic over red lights, I am sure most Germans would rather vote for the latter, considering the technical signals require less coordinating with other drivers, which also means less swearing and lecturing others on road traffic regulations! When it comes to showing emotions, a thumb rule is that Germans sing in the shower and go hog wild in the car; *Have you won your license on the lottery!* is a comparably lenient common abuse.

If you do not have to go someplace in the countryside, there is no need to rent a car. Take a train, planning enough of a buffer for delays (100 percent on time arrival is a myth), and ask for help at the *Deutsche Bahn Service Centers* to find the best possible routes and connections. Otherwise, use www.bahn.de or the DB App to plan your journey and buy your ticket. Not every taxi driver would be able or willing to accept credit cards, so enquire in advance and make sure you carry enough euros (EUR, €). Tariffs vary from city to city and, unless fixed prices for very standard routes (from the airport to the city center or fairground, for example) are advertised, you pay by taxi meter.

If your chauffeur is a native German, chances are that the person who, at the end of the journey, will be happy to issue a hand-written receipt for your cash payment (add a small tip, if you like) has a diploma in psychology, theology, or some other social-scientific discipline. Having lost track on their career path while studying German philology, politics, or some other exotic "Blütenfach" (literal: flower subject) for some 14 or 16 semesters (i.e., seven or eight years), your cabbie might have chosen to keep on driving a car to earn a living, rather than trying to fit into the corporate or academic world. With the "Americanization" of the university system, as some would put it, youngsters these days have fewer opportunities to come true in disciplines that have no concrete value. Nowadays, qualification (fitness for purpose) ranks higher than a holistic education, but that is another story.

Talking to your driver might be a good opportunity for you to get an idea about what is going to expect you when you are meeting your business prospects. Firstly, your taxi ride might give you a foretaste of how blunt Germans can be. Although, in Germany, talking about your own political preferences would be considered a taboo topic—now that I think about it, maybe that has changed slightly in recent years—do not be surprised if your driver is happy to share his or her views on the politics of the day in *your* country.

The driver might also lecture you about how you have chosen a lousy or overpriced hotel; if it is also slightly difficult to reach the place (because of one-way streets or road works) or the length of the journey (i.e., the fare) does not offset the time the driver had to queue up at the airport or station, you are likely to be educated on the inconvenience caused to him or her. I once took a cab to transport an oriental-style coffee table I had just purchased from an inexpensive antique shop; while helping me to unload the table from his trunk (at least!), the driver's very matter-of-fact comment was: "Hopefully, you haven't paid any money for this crappy piece of bulk trash." And, please note that I only remember the episode because he spoilt the excitement I had felt, not because my taste had been questioned by a total stranger!

When it comes to small talk, the weather is always a safe topic. Germans, being used to complaining a lot, would often tell you that it is too hot, too cold, too rainy, too cloudy, too sunny, but I would say that the weather conditions in Germany overall are quite pleasant and easily bearable, if you are dressed accordingly. Abhilash V R, a principal design engineer from South India who experienced the quite exceptional –16 degrees Celsius (3.2 Fahrenheit) when he first came to Germany for a fair in February 2018, would most certainly agree when I say that you had better buy or bring proper shoes and a warm coat for the winter (northern hemisphere: December–March); and do not be surprised to experience up to 30 degrees Celsius (86 Fahrenheit) in the summer. However, air conditioning is not very commonly used and, unless your meeting is taking place in some very modern and well-equipped building, you might quickly feel tempted to undo your tie. In winters, sitting in overheated offices might make you regret the decision to wear a woolen, long-sleeve shirt and boots with your knee length business outfit! So far, we have not experienced monsoons or hurricanes, and blizzards are not exactly common; however, sometimes there are storms and flooding.

Talking about flooding, you might be wondering what the small badge in the front of the taxi is supposed to be; some cars have a silver token attached to the car's dashboard, close to the steering wheel (which, by the way, is on the left-hand side of the car). The emblem depicts a man with a long walking stick, who is carrying a child on his shoulders; both are surrounded by rough waters. You might already have guessed that the child is Jesus. The man carrying the Christ Child is St. Christopher, the patron saint of travelers, as well as car conductors; rafts men; and truck, bus, and taxi drivers. Your driver is very likely to be a Catholic.

However, religion does not play a major role in Germany. According to data published by *fowid,* only 37 percent say that religion and belief are of high or very high importance to them (Frerk 2017). In the cited survey, which was conducted by *Infratest dimap* in 2017, 63 percent of the interviewees responded that religion played a minor role or no role at all in their lives. Overall, women are often more religious than men, and the people living in the western parts of Germany are more religious than those living in the eastern parts of the country. According to *fowid,* 36.2 percent of the Germans do not follow any religion, while Roman Catholics account for 28.5 percent of the population and 26.5 percent are Protestants. There are about 4.9 percent Muslims and 3.9 percent who belong to other churches or follow other beliefs. The communities that are growing are Muslims (due to the recent influx of immigrants, especially from Syria and Afghanistan), people who follow no religion at all, and those from other beliefs or churches (Forschungsgruppe Weltanschauungen in Deutschland und der Welt (fowid) 2017).

As surveys show, there are many things that are, on an average, more important to Germans than religion. Health, family or children, and friendship rank much higher, as do education, work or occupation, and nature (Frerk 2017). When Germans talk about the importance of family, most often, they are referring to (their) nuclear family, typically consisting of themselves, their partner, and one or two children. They would also consider their parents and siblings as close family, maybe along with their grandparents. Aunts, uncles, and cousins often would not really be considered family, and when it comes to great-aunts, co-brothers-in-law, or second cousins, many would not even know the terms! It would also never occur to autochthonous (indigenous) Germans to call their parents' friends "uncle" and "aunt," or address the vegetable vendor as "brother" or "sister." The only person who is not blood-related to me and whom I address as "uncle" is my godfather (Patenonkel), Peter; and I call my late father's sister's late husband's second cousin's son Amit and his first cousin Arjun "cousins," but that's another story, because that is India!

As you can see in Table 1.2 (Federal Statistical Office n.d.), in 2017, about 42 percent of the 41.3 million households in Germany were one-person households; 59 percent of all Germans were either married or living together (Statista GmbH, Hamburg 2018b). Living together without being married is socially accepted, and most couples, when they tie the knot, have already lived together for some time. The current divorce rate is roughly 40 percent, meaning that, for each marriage, there are 0.4 divorces. Or, if I am getting the numbers right, one could also say that two out of five couples get divorced. Many of my friends live in patchwork families, and common questions are whether or not to invite the ex-wife to their daughter's graduation party, and what weekends the new boyfriend is in charge of taking the kids.

By the way, it is better not to ask your German business contacts about their marital status or whether they have children. Most Germans, at least at an early stage of getting to know each other, would perceive these questions as being far too personal; for an unmarried person or somebody without children, the question might even sound like an insult. If people mention their children by themselves, then it is a very good idea to inquire how the offspring are doing, what their hobbies

Table 1.2 Key figures on households and families, 2017

Households	41.3 mn
One-person households	41.8%
Families with minor children	8.2 mn
Married couples	69.7%
Lone parents	18.9%
Cohabiting couples	11.4%
Couples	20.8 mn
Married couples	84.4%
Opposite-sex cohabiting couples	15.0%
Same-sex cohabiting couples	0.5%

are, and whether they already know what profession they would like to follow.

(Industry) Clusters and the Relevance of the Mittelstand

Would you be able to name five to 10 German brands or companies? Most probably, you know or would have at least heard of Adidas, Allianz, Deutsche Lufthansa, BMW, Volkswagen (VW), SAP, and Siemens. The *Nivea* logo on the little blue tin in your cosmetics cabinet represents a world-famous body-care brand owned by Hamburg-based Beiersdorf. *Audi* as well as *Porsche* belong to the Volkswagen Group. According to Interbrand, a global brand consulting agency, in 2017, *Mercedes-Benz* (The Daimler Group) ranked the highest when it came to the most valuable German brands (ninth worldwide) (Interbrand n.d.).

The aforementioned companies are all (currently) listed on the German stock index *DAX* (Deutscher Aktienindex), which consists of the 30 major German companies trading on the Frankfurt Stock Exchange. However, the backbone of the German economy is the so-called *Mittelstand.* Mittelstand, in German-speaking countries (Germany, Austria, and parts of Switzerland), *commonly* refers to small- and medium-sized enterprises (SMEs) with annual revenues of up to 50 million euros and a maximum of 499 employees (Institut für Mittelstandsforschung Bonn n.d.). Depending on its *specific* definition, "Mittelstand" can range all the way from small craft workshops to hidden champions worth up to a billion euros.[1]

According to the online portal *Die Deutsche Wirtschaft*, the Mittelstand not only accounts for the majority of businesses in Germany (more than three million), but also provides some 60 percent of all jobs and

---

[1] Billion as in 10^9; that is, in German, "eine Milliarde." Please be careful when discussing numbers with a person who speaks German. In German, "eine Billion" is what people from the United States would call trillion. And, while we are on the subject, do not be confused by how Germans space numbers; up to a billion euros would be written as "up to EUR 1.000.000.000" or, if you would like to add 50 cents, "EUR 1.000.000.000,50."

over 80 percent of all apprenticeships. A study conducted by the portal has analyzed Germany's most important medium-sized companies (Die Deutsche Wirtschaft 2016):

> *The results provide an interesting insight into the structure, distribution and relevance of the most important medium-sized companies in Germany. In this respect, turnover at the top 10,000 firms ranges from approximately 25 million to the ranking limit of 1 billion euros. The average turnover is 156 million euros. All in all, the top 10,000 companies account for roughly 1.05 billion euros in turnover and provide approximately 5.3 million jobs.*

Die Deutsche Wirtschaft also found that most of the top companies are from the automotive trade, followed by mechanical engineering and construction. According to their research, 56 percent are to be classified as industry, 27 percent as service providers, and 17 percent as retailers (ibid). When ranked according to federal state, the largest number of the medium-sized enterprises (as described above) is currently based in North Rhine-Westphalia (2,300), followed by Bavaria (1,997) and Baden-Wuerttemberg (1,812) (Die Deutsche Wirtschaft 2018).

The portal regularly publishes their ranking of the most important SMEs (Table 1.3); in addition to the turnover and number of employees, they attach weight to research collaborations, partnerships with schools or universities, and association memberships (Die Deutsche Wirtschaft 2016).

Looking at where the below top 25 companies are located, you might notice that there is only one big city listed—Berlin. Maybe you have heard of Bremen (about 550,000 inhabitants) or Wiesbaden (275,000). Fridolfing, for example, where Rosenberger Hochfrequenztechnik is located, is home to about 4,200 people; Klingenberg am Main, where we find WIKA, is not much bigger. I am telling you this because, in my experience and due to a common misconception, some people conduct their Internet search for potential business partners or buyers only by city: Berlin, Hamburg, Munich, and so on. Sometimes, maybe because of how they experience centralism or the infrastructure in their home countries,

Table 1.3 The top 25 of the 10,000 most important medium-sized companies as per Die Deutsche Wirtschaft

Rank	Company name	City or location	Industry	Turnover in mn EUR
1	ifm stiftung & Co KG	Essen	Automation engineering	815
2	Maschinenfabrik Reinhausen GmbH	Regensburg	Electrical engineering	700
3	Borgers SE & Co. KGaA	Bocholt	Automotive supplier	823
4	C. D. Wälzholz KG	Hagen	Steel processing	850
5	Windmöller & Hölscher Gruppe	Lengerich	Machine engineering	785
6	apetito AG	Rheine	Foodstuff	829
7	WIKA Alexander Wiegand SE & Co. KG	Klingenberg	Control technology	834
8	Kathrein-Gruppe	Rosenheim	Communication technology	794
9	Schnellecke Group AG & Co. KG	Wolfsburg	Automobile logistics	936
10	Rosenberger Hochfrequenztechnik GmbH & Co KG	Fridolfing	Electrical engineering	940
11	MEWA Textil-Service AG & Co. Management OHG	Wiesbaden	Textile or textile services	638
12	Dehner Holding GmbH & Co. KG	Rain am Lech	Garden market	781
13	Unternehmensgruppe Lürssen	Bremen	Dockyards	985
14	dennree Gruppe	Töpen	Wholesale organic food	920
15	Beumer Group GmbH & Co. KG	Beckum	Machinery and plant engineering	750
16	Gegenbauer Holding SE & Co. KG	Berlin	Facility management	685
17	Lindner Group KG	Arnstorf	Building or building materials	950
18	Schön Klinik SE	Prien a. Chiemsee	Health	797

19	WAGO Kontakttechnik GmbH & Co. KG	Minden	Connection technologies and automation	766
20	Max Weishaupt GmbH	Schwendi	Building technology	560
21	Handtmann Unternehmensgruppe	Biberach	Machine engineering	835
22	Harting AG & Co. KG	Espelkamp	Industrial connectors	586
23	Bitburger Braugruppe GmbH	Bitburg	Breweries	785
24	WITTE Automotive	Velbert	Automotive supplier	595
25	HiPP Gruppe	Pfaffenhofen	Foodstuff	950

foreigners imagine that businesses would only flourish within major cities or their exurbs. That is *not* the case with Germany!

However, it is very important to grasp the regional differences when starting to do business or working on business development in Germany. A business consultant in my network would often encourage companies to focus on just one region when entering the German market, depending on the product in question, the industrial competence of the region itself, and other factors. There are regions where specific competences are aggregated and certain skills or industries have been flourishing for centuries, whereas there are (newer) cluster networks that are often funded by the federal government and federal states to promote certain technologies.

In his book, *Hidden Champions – Aufbruch nach Globalia*, management consultant and Emeritus Professor of Economics Hermann Simon distinguishes three kinds of industry clusters. Traditional clusters, among others, subsume the retail sector. In the region of Mühlheim / Essen, for example, you would find many retail companies. Solingen is famous for cutlery; roller bearings are produced in and around Schweinfurt; and Nuremberg is the place where you would find the most important pencil manufacturers. Clusters of companies that are specializing in what Simon calls "ripe" products or technologies are, for example, manufacturers of surgical instruments (Tuttlingen), ventilation (Hohenlohe), or metal bending (Siegen / Haiger). The registered society *Measurement Valley* (Göttingen) currently comprises about 40 companies and organizations from their respective industries and, while Simon uses the term "Chicken Valley" for the city of Vechta, the local people, according to my cursory research, seem to more often refer to the region as the "Silicon Valley of Agricultural Technology." Looking at the clusters for early stage technologies, Simon (2012, pp. 60–62) mentions recycling (Karlsruhe / Essingen) and carbon fiber (Munich / Augsburg / Ingolstadt). The author has also observed that there are small towns like Neutraubling and Künzelsau that seem to provide a breeding ground for a viral entrepreneurial spirit and an infectious inventive mind.

To identify those regions or clusters that are especially relevant for your purposes, you could peruse the online platform https://clusterplattform.de that is operated by the Federal Ministry for Economic Affairs and Energy. You could also double-check how *Germany Trade and Invest's* (GTAI's) website http://gtai.de can be helpful for your research. GTAI offers in-depth information on the economic structure of Germany for each federal state. Another website that I can recommend in this context: https://make-it-in-germany.com.

If you are an investor, I suggest that you, at some stage in the process, also get in touch with the business promotion agencies of the various states, such as *Invest in Bavaria* or *IMG – Investment and Marketing Corporation Saxony-Anhalt*. Some of the things you can ask them to help you include finding office space or connecting you to lawyers and tax consultants. Many (if not all) of their services are free of charge.

You would still find the highest concentration of (successful) SMEs in the West of Germany; after almost 30 years of German unification, there continue to be major structural differences. Table 1.4 shows the distribution of the top 10,000 SMEs by federal state, as researched by *Die Deutsche Wirtschaft* (2018). I have added the English language names of the federal states and the names of the state capitals for your convenience. I have also embedded information on whether the states belonged to East or West Germany between 1949 and 1990.

Table 1.4 Federal states ranking of the top 10,000 SMEs as per Die Deutsche Wirtschaft

Rank	Federal state (German / English)	(Former) East or West?	Capital (German / English)	Number of top 10,000 medium-sized companies
1	Nordrhein-Westfalen / North Rhine-Westphalia	West	Düsseldorf / Dusseldorf	2,288
2	(Freistaat) Bayern / (The Free State of) Bavaria	West	München / Munich	1,970
3	Baden-Württemberg / Baden-Wuerttemberg	West	Stuttgart / Stuttgart	1,819
4	Niedersachsen / Lower Saxony	West	Hannover / Hanover	988
5	Hessen / Hesse	West	Wiesbaden / Wiesbaden	554
6	Rheinland-Pfalz / Rhineland-Palatinate	West	Mainz / Mainz	397
7	Hamburg / Hamburg	West	Hamburg / Hamburg	356
8	Schleswig-Holstein / Schleswig-Holstein	West	Kiel / Kiel	348
9	(Freistaat) Sachsen / (The Free State of) Saxony	East	Dresden / Dresden	329
10	Berlin / Berlin	Formerly divided city (East and West)	Berlin / Berlin	263
11	(Freistaat) Thüringen / (The Free State of) Thuringia	East	Erfurt / Erfurt	159
12	Sachsen-Anhalt / Saxony-Anhalt	East	Magdeburg / Magdeburg	133
13	Bremen / Bremen	West	Bremen / Bremen	119
14	Brandenburg / Brandenburg	East	Potsdam / Potsdam	115
15	Saarland / Saarland	West	Saarbrücken / Saarbrücken	90
16	Mecklenburg-Vorpommern / Mecklenburg-Western Pomerania	East	Schwerin / Schwerin	72

According to the Federal Ministry of Education and Research, the new German Länder[2] Brandenburg, Mecklenburg-Western Pomerania, Saxony, Saxony-Anhalt, and Thuringia primarily lack large research-based companies and mid-sized companies that are experienced in the global marketplace. An entrepreneurial funding policy has, therefore, been established. Investors are often attracted by reduced local business taxes; the municipal tax factor can play a major role when making your FDI decision, especially when choosing a location to set up shop!

Regional Peculiarities

Stewart Siegel, an international technical director from the United States living in Germany, finds the regional differences "pretty drastic." However, he is "not sure even all Germans understand the differences themselves." Apart from the landscape, industries, infrastructure, and the tax factor, would you be able to observe any (other) disparities?

Baden-Wurttemberg's slogan "Wir können alles. Außer Hochdeutsch" (We can do everything, except speak proper High German) in a self-deprecating manner sums up how the people of the state (or their ad agency) like to see themselves:

> *Poor in natural resources, the population is overflowing with ingenuity, inventive spirit and an appetite for hard work. The creativity and ingenuity of its people, their skill and expertise, their commitment to industry, science, education, culture and society have made Germany's Southwest one of the world's most successful regions.*

We can read this in the state's online presence (Staatsministerium Baden-Württemberg n.d.). The Swabian dialect is indeed somewhat extraordinary, but dialects themselves are omnipresent. Language is something that greatly varies within Germany, although all native Germans should be able to speak proper High German at some advanced level. Apart from the dialect (certain terms we use), the tonality or ductus greatly varies.

---

[2] "*New* German Länder" (*neue* Bundesländer) is what we—or at least many—still call the states from former East Germany.

The background noise in public transportation, for example, sounds very different depending on which place you are in. People in Hamburg are comparably soft-spoken and, to me, sound more sophisticated and distinguished than people in many other parts of Germany. In Berlin (the "poor, but sexy" city, quoting former mayor Klaus Wowereit), you do not need to be able to follow the accent to get the message(s). Snippy or detached comments hit your face like hailstorms; when you check in to your hotel, for example. I had never noticed how rude my Bavarian dialect possibly sounds (especially for a foreigner), until I sensed how one of my international clients froze in shock when I spoke to (or barked at) a local trade show visitor during a major building and construction fair in Munich.

A lot of things are in the responsibility of the 16 states and influence peoples' lives from the womb to the tomb; although, at that last stage, you might not exactly care about the local regulations on the obligatory inspection of the (your) corpse any more. For example, the timings of school holidays can vary from state to state, and you might want to take this into account when planning your business trip to Germany, especially during the summer. Police is also of federal concern. Very recently, the Bavarian police ventured out to Munich airport to track down families who wanted to go on holiday even though the school break had not yet officially started; 10 parents were fined. You may also take this as an example of Germans' appreciation for rules, regulations, and structures—even if people do not always go by the rulebook.

Shop opening hours can greatly vary, although, so far, shops across Germany are not allowed to open on Sunday or on (regional) bank holidays. In the more conservative southern state of Bavaria, shops are allowed to be open between 6 a.m. and 8 p.m., while in Saxony, people can (theoretically) grocery shop until 10 p.m.; that shopkeepers can keep their stores open around the clock in many other German states feels alien to me! If *I* want to buy toiletries or something to eat after 8 p.m., I need to head for the Munich central terminal or the nearest gas station. On the other hand, in some rural and neglected areas, especially in the east, people do not have any shops to go to any more, let alone train stations, post offices, or hospitals! For the size and number of inhabitants of the various states, refer to Table 1.5 (Statistisches Bundesamt 2018b). I have sorted the federal states by the size of the territory.

Table 1.5 Federal states size and number of inhabitants as of December 31, 2016[3]

Federal state	Size of the territory (sq km)	Population	
		Altogether	Per sq km
Bayern	70,542	12,930,751	183
Niedersachsen	47,710	7,945,685	167
Baden-Württemberg	35,749	10,951,893	306
Nordrhein-Westfalen	34,113	17,890,100	524
Brandenburg	29,654	2,494,648	84
Mecklenburg-Vorpommern	23,294	1,610,674	69
Hessen	21,115	6,213,088	294
Sachsen-Anhalt	20,452	2,236,252	109
Rheinland-Pfalz	19,858	4,066,053	205
Sachsen	18,450	4,081,783	221
Thüringen	16,202	2,158,128	133
Schleswig-Holstein	15,802	2,881,926	182
Saarland	2,571	996,651	388
Berlin	891	3,574,830	4,012
Hamburg	755	1,810,438	2,397
Bremen	419	678,753	1,617
Germany	**357,578**	**82,521,653**	**231**

Food is also something that varies from region to region. What I have noticed, apart from culinary specialties, is that, when I am in a restaurant in Cologne (Köln), the choice of vegetarian dishes is smaller than that in where I live. And, the beer comes in smaller glasses! I have also observed that people in Cologne like to talk a lot. While the natives of Munich are happy to mutter into their one-liter jugs, people from Cologne would rather order and share one so-called Kranz (wreath) of 0.2 liter glasses after another.

[3] The data concerning the overall size of Germany does not exactly match the number given at the start of the chapter, and it also differs from other sources. The federal statistics office in a footnote (among other things) explains that, due to technical and methodical adjustments in the surveying administration, the comparison of area data from 2014 onward with the area data from previous years is only possible to a limited extent (Statistisches Bundesamt 2018b).

If you are traveling to Germany for business, do not neglect regional holidays and the so-called "fifth(s) season(s) of the year." During the "crazy days" of the Cologne Carnival, you might not be able to arrange for a *single* business meeting, and when you try to book a hotel room during Munich Oktoberfest, be ready to be charged a fat premium.

Much-traveled consultant Alexander Wurz points out that the regional differences in Germany "are stronger than in many other countries due to our history." One should remember "that we had, in 1648, over 350 more or less autonomous states, kingdoms, and independent duchies, and that Germany has been a nation only since 1871." Maybe that is also a reason why Germans are sometimes so biased about their neighbors. I once mentioned to a client in Bremen that I was especially looking forward to visiting Hamburg (about 125 km to go). Big mistake! I soon learned that, for a long time, people in Bremen have been suffering from some inferiority complex toward Hamburg (HH). For intercultural coach Andrew MacKichan, who has grown up in the UK, it "was quite a shock to discover that the HH people can't stand the Bavarians." And my friend Tina Oreskovich, a service delivery manager from Würzburg, a region that has not exactly voluntarily joined the Free State of Bavaria (short: Bavaria), adds: "Franconians are not Bavarians!"

This reminds me of how I, as a child, once overheard a conversation in which a major scandal was being discussed: a girl from Catholic Lower Bavaria had wed a Protestant from Franconia (*a Lutheran, God forbid!*). But that must have been some 35 years ago, and things are changing in Germany—like everywhere else. Most probably, these specific regional differences and animosities are not so crucial for foreigners and become secondary when dealing with Germany's international top companies anyway. If you want to move to Germany, or an expat position is offered to you, you might want to double-check, however.

CHAPTER 2

What You Should Know About (Our) History

Be Aware of Biased Viewpoints

Whatever people (myself included) tell you about history, always bear in mind that their views could, at least to some extent, be biased. The way we look at the world, including history, is greatly influenced by what we have been told by our parents, school teachers, or colleagues, and so on. What is printed in the newspapers and broadcasted on the TV does shape our minds and even our collective memory.

I can only vaguely remember what my teachers were talking about in history class. It's not that I was an ignorant child; being a binge reader, I couldn't help but incidentally learn about the past—from a white and Western perspective, I might add! In the second grade, I was the best pupil in class, and as a reward, I recall the school giving me a book of adventure stories about a boy in some jungle. Looking at what (ethnocentric nonsense) is *still* commonly presented to our kids (Riemhofer 2014), I guess the smart white boy must have taught some not-so-smart indigenous kids how to meet the (everyday) challenges of jungle life. At the age of 10 or 12 years, I had already consumed page-turners like *Gone with the Wind*, *Papillon*, and *The Thorn Birds*. Maybe because of my nine-years staying at a Catholic convent boarding school, I could especially identify with (fictional) autobiographies dealing with prison breaks or an escape from (Russian) war captivity. A novel that greatly helped me develop an idea of Germany's most inglorious period was Judith Kerr's *When Hitler Stole Pink Rabbit*.

Patchwork Central Europe and the Power of the Church

History class was nothing like that. History class was—as far as *I* remember—for the most part, an endless exercise of filling notebooks, line by line, with years of wars, dates of battles, and the names of the ruling houses having the upper hand in patchwork Central Europe at the respective times. In a nutshell, the region, for hundreds of years, consisted of numerous microstates, church lands, and free cities. There was a lot of fighting going on; if it was opportune, enemies would become (temporary) allies. The territorial fragmentation (*Kleinstaaterei*) resulted in the current regionalism, which, as discussed in Chapter 1, influences many aspects of peoples' lives and how they do business even today.

From what I understand, we have always been in a love-hate relationship with the French, whom we secretly admire(d) for their civilized behavior and savoir vivre. For many centuries, it was a common practice that aristocrats, especially in the diplomatic field, would rather converse in French than in the contemporary German (dialects). However, my brother recently wondered why, at school, his daughter should learn French over Spanish, when many more people worldwide speak Spanish. My guess is that the preference for (still) teaching our neighbors' language greatly relates to the *Franco-German Friendship Treaty* signed by President Charles de Gaulle (1890–1970) and Chancellor Konrad Adenauer (1876–1967) in 1963.

Charles the Great (748–814 AD), King of the Franks and ruler of most of what is now France and Germany, had (already) united much of western and central Europe during the early Middle Ages. The French call him Charlemagne and the Germans know him as "Karl der Große." He is said to have been revered by his contemporaries as the "Father of Europe," and since 1950, the *International Charlemagne Prize of Aachen* (Germany) honors exceptional work performed in the service of European unity. In 2018, the award was presented to the President of the French Republic, Emmanuel Macron, in recognition of his vision of a new Europe and the re-establishment of the European project (Stiftung Internationaler Karlspreis zu Aachen 2018). During Charlemagne's time, Christianizing, upon penalty of death if a baptism was refused, was the means of choice to forcefully promote the idea.

The Roman Catholic Church has always played a major role in the history of Europe and the so-called *Holy Roman Empire*. In fact, for centuries, it was the pope who crowned the emperors. Therefore, it was crucial for the royal candidates to be allowed to participate in the sacraments of the Church in the first place. You might have heard of the (proverbial) *Walk to Canossa* (*Gang nach Canossa*); to seek absolution for his excommunication, disgraced 26-year-old Holy Roman Emperor Henry IV (1050–1106) whipped on a penitential robe, crossed the Alps, and traveled to Canossa Castle, Italy, where Pope Gregory VII was staying at the time. According to contemporary sources, the emperor was forced to humiliate himself, waiting barefoot in front of the castle gate for three days and nights in cold and stormy weather. Depending on your perspective, you may call the episode a great strategic move or view it as a most embarrassing mortification. What I would like to highlight is that the concept of asking for forgiveness, in my experience, is very common and highly appreciated in Germany. While people from many other cultures might perceive "I am deeply sorry" as an act of self-humiliation or loss of face, Germans would often expect an explicit apology as a matter of common decency.

In the early modern period, when the greater part of the population was terrified by the prospect of burning in hell for their dark and dirty deeds, the act of forgiveness was even marketed: after confessing, or in exchange for doing godly work, the faithful received a decree exempting them from punishment for their sins. Letters of indulgence were also sold by the Catholic Church to finance the building of cathedrals or going to war, for example. In 1517, a monk from Eisleben sparked the Reformation by compiling a document that attacked the Catholic Church for this practice. To publish them, he is said to have nailed his 95 theses to the door of the Wittenberg Castle Church. As a professor of Moral Theology, Martin Luther (1483–1546) argued that the practice of selling indulgence letters led Christians to overlook true repentance and sorrow for their sins; he reasoned the habit discouraged them from giving to the poor and performing other acts of mercy, believing that indulgence certificates were more spiritually valuable (Deutsche Nationalbibliothek n.d.). Thanks to the quite newly invented printing press (c. 1440), Luther's writings had a wide reach and greatly influenced the religious and cultural history in Europe: The Reformation resulted in the split of the Roman Catholic Church and the birth of Protestantism. It led to wars and persecution, but also to greater freedom of religion and expression. During the recent 500th anniversary celebrations, Luther was also greatly honored for his translating the Word of God for/to the common man. So far, with some exceptions, mainly Latin and Greek versions of the Book had been available; texts could be read (hence, interpreted) by only very educated people such as churchmen. In translating the Bible, the linguistic genius Luther not only gave people easy access to so far "classified information," but also invented a very vivid (common) language and created many figurative expressions that we still use. Some, I believe, are now even common in other languages, as, for example, "Ein Buch mit sieben Siegeln" (a book of seven seals) to describe something that—for you—is an incomprehensible, difficult-to-access subject matter (like quantum physics, or understanding the opposite sex, maybe).

"Great" Wars and the (First) German Nation

After the Reformation came the Counter-Reformation, and—in and around the territory—a series of (religious) conflicts and other revolts termed the *Dreißigjähriger Krieg* (1618–1648), which is *still* somehow present in the collective memory of the Germans. In the so-called Thirty Years' War, people were not only falling on the battlefields, but the population was also dropping like flies from famines and epidemic plagues. In some places, two-thirds of the people died, and some regions are said to have needed more than 100 years to recover from the consequences of the war. However, the recollection of the endured misery was certainly not strong enough to prevent our folks from inciting other wars![1]

Under this heading, let us fast-forward to the end of the 19th century: after conquering Denmark and Austria, we—Prussia and some southern states—were fighting the French yet again; they had started the war in 1870 after receiving an offensive letter that had been modified (one could maybe even say "manipulated") by the Minister President of Prussia, Otto von Bismarck (1815–1898). This time, France had to suffer defeat, and based on the success story, Bismarck slowly managed to convince the other German states (which were kingdoms and grand duchies) to enter a confederation under Prussian leadership. Bismarck became the

---

[1] Rather was one "lesson learned" for later warlords to seek not to engage in a war of exhaustion (again), but rather try to quickly subdue invaded territories.

Imperial Chancellor. The King of Prussia, Wilhelm Friedrich Ludwig of Hohenzollern, short name William I (1797–1888), who was not exactly excited about the additional job, was declared the German Emperor. In January 1871, the German "Kaiserreich" was proclaimed in the Palace of Versailles (France) and stretched from the Rhine to Russia. The palace's Hall of Mirrors would, over time, become a very symbolic place for the "ups and downs" (if one can use this expression) of the newly heralded, overly self-confident, and self-conscious German Empire.

The following excerpt from a booklet that was published for British Servicemen in 1944 reflects a foreign (maybe more precisely, British) perspective on what happened next (The Foreign Office, London 2014, p. 12):

> *The vices of militarism and aggressiveness, often thought to be peculiar to the Prussians, soon infected the whole of Germany. The Germans acquired colonies, chiefly in Africa; they challenged the British sea-power by building a powerful fleet. And in 1914 they thought they were strong enough to enforce an unchallenged supremacy in Europe. In alliance with Austria-Hungary, Turkey and Bulgaria they fought and lost the First World War.*

As we can see, the story did not end in favor of the Germans and the *Treaty of Versailles*, signed in the aforementioned Hall of Mirrors, compelled the Germans to pay extensive war reparations. Many people grew desperate, especially when the Great Depression struck Germany even harder than other countries in the 1920s. At times, almost half the working population was unemployed; women (who had only recently gained the right to vote) were soon urged to give up their jobs and return home to their traditional roles as wives and mothers.

I vividly remember my grandparents' stories about hyperinflation, when a loaf of bread easily cost billions of Mark and how, on payday, people would rush to the stores to get rid of their bank notes as quickly as possible. They had to use wash baskets or towing vehicles to carry their money.

The fear of unemployment and depreciation of money still manifests in peoples' minds. While the level of debt has recently been rising alarmingly in the millennial generation (those born around the year 2000), in my own generation (which is only 20–30 years older), putting aside money before making a private investment (like buying a car or remodeling a kitchen) is still the preferred practice. Credit cards are not extensively used, and overall, people would rather not risk not being able to pay their respective bills. Also, Germans are not very fond of job-hopping, and maybe this is also due to this collective memory. What I find hard to digest is that, until the 1970s, in the Federal Republic of Germany, a wife needed her husband's (written) consent if she wanted to work!

Nazi Germany and the Preliminaries of the Second World War

The Great Depression was an ideal breeding ground for the rise of the National Socialist German Worker's Party NSDAP under Adolf Hitler (1889–1945). One of the Nazis' alluring promises was to wipe out the Treaty of Versailles, and in doing so, not only heal the wounds of the perceived humiliation, but also make Germany great (or, significant) again. In a hidden agenda to prepare Germany for war, the regime invested heavily in the expansion of industry and infrastructure. Watching professionally staged propaganda films displaying healthy, heroic workers constructing the German highways (Autobahn), Hitler must have appeared a savior to many people. To some extent, that knowledge might help to grasp the leader cult (*Führerkult*) and the collective hysteria of the time. I always get the creeps when I watch footage of Hitler giving public speeches; according to the (propagandistic) film documents, some women even fainted from excitement. It makes my skin crawl when I observe how, lately, politicians (no matter from which party) increasingly use an aggressive tone, sometimes even shouting their requests in what reminds me of the common staccato popular in the "old times." I can understand the parallels to the sentiments during the Weimar Republic that are described by some critical observers like, for example, the political scientist Max Czollek (2018). Maybe, based on these discussions, Germany's early dropout from the FIFA World Championships in 2018 made me feel less uncomfortable than the sight of the then (and once again) fashionable undercut hairstyles sported by some of the tall, blond (Nordic) players. What has always caused me the greatest level of discomfort is when, even in a business context, I meet foreigners who want to engage me in a conversation about the "great leadership" skills of one of the greatest brutes the world has ever seen.

In the 1930s, almost every household had a *Volksempfänger* ("Volk" like "folk," as in *Volkswagen*) that must have tremendously helped brainwashing the people, especially because you were not allowed to listen to stations other than those operated or endorsed by the regime. You better did not tell your neighbor when you violated the provision; you never knew if he or she would denounce you to the *Blockwart* (local group leader).

Hitler made people feel valued and important; everyone in line with the Nazi ideology was equipped with a uniform or a medal and could feel at home in some organization fitting his or her role in the Reich: boys were brought into line in the *Hitlerjugend* (HJ, Hitler Youth), while girls enjoyed activities and companionship in the *Bund Deutscher Mädel* (BDM, League of German Girls). It was the healthy, Aryan women's duty to "dem Führer Kinder zu schenken" (gift the Führer children), and there was a sophisticated reward system for living births: depending on the number of children, the mother was rewarded with a certain rank of the *Cross of Honor for the German Mother*: third rank *Mutterkreuz* for four or five kids, second for six or seven kids, and first for eight or more!

Appointed Imperial Chancellor (*Reichskanzler*) in 1933, Hitler quickly managed to silence the people or parties that would oppose him and established a dictatorship with him as "Leader" (Führer) *and* "Reich" Chancellor. "Then he began to 'discipline' the country," we read in the *Instructions for British Servicemen in Germany,* issued by the Foreign Office, London, in 1944 (p. 14): "Law was suspended. Jews, Communists, Socialists, Liberals—anyone who had publicly opposed him—were hunted down by Hitler's private army, the Storm Troops, shot, beaten to death, or systematically tortured in concentration camps." In the booklet, it is highlighted that "Hitler's aim was so to terrorise the German people that no one would dare to resist him by deed or word."

Reflecting upon it, one could argue that questioning hierarchy and opposing rulers is not exactly, or at least was not, a strong tradition in Germany at the time. Rather, people had, for centuries, been trained to be subservient to authority and blindly execute demands, no matter how cruel or stupid they were. Heinrich Mann (1871–1950) has described the subordinate type in his novel *Der Untertan* (The Loyal Subject), published in 1914. Neither making decisions nor assuming responsibilities has been *truly* German virtues, and the "subordinate trait" is still somehow prevalent in the German society. I recently met a lady from France, who has known (West) Germany since her student days in the 1980s; having lived and worked in the country for more than 20 years now, she has often observed what she calls the "German paradox":

> *I feel that while, on the one hand, people are courageous enough to express their opinion—you see students freely expressing their ideas and asking questions, and even challenging their professor in the main auditorium, on the other hand, Germans would rather hide behind hierarchy when it comes to taking up a responsibility; such as, when at work, taking up a specific task that is not mentioned in the job description.*
>
> *And, if during a convention or closed conference, someone from upper management shares the breakfast or dinner table with a group, most Germans listen religiously to the words spoken by that upper manager and don't dare expressing a different opinion and debating.*

Trying to hide behind hierarchy was also a popular argumentation strategy after the war: "Not my fault, I was only obeying orders" was the bottom line of the pardon plea of one of the major organizers of the Holocaust, Adolf Eichmann (1906–1962), written shortly before he was about to be executed for his war crimes in Israel. Back in Nazi Germany, more than just the people not in favor of Hitler and his regime were chased, and Eichmann was one of the key people taking care of the logistics. During the Holocaust, the Nazi regime and its collaborators systematically not only persecuted and murdered six million Jews, but—and the following list is *still* not complete—also targeted Sinti and Roma, disabled people, communists, socialists, members of the resistance, Jehovah's Witnesses, and homosexuals. According to latest research, the Holocaust may have claimed up to 20 million lives (Day 2013).

How all this could have happened was not a question extensively discussed *immediately* after the end of the war, when Germans were busy re-establishing their existences and mourning their personal losses. Only in 1968, when university campuses all over the world transformed into battlegrounds for social change, German students did begin to openly accuse and oppose the older generation for tolerating some of the former members of the Nazi Party in key political roles (Schaefer 2008). Until then, discussing war crimes had not been on the class schedule.

The broadcast of the American mini-series, *Holocaust,* in the Federal Republic in 1979 for many was the turning point for Germany's willingness to look (closely) at and discuss their history. Some historians call the TV program and subsequent discussions, watched by about 50 percent (!) of West Germans, a milestone in the German history of mentality. Finally, the common people were ready to (publicly) ask about and dispute their inglorious history; I remember my confusion when my mother (born in the early 1950s) tried to talk to me about how mothers and their children were gassed in what looked like showers. That must have been shortly after the first screening of *Holocaust* and was most probably a matter far too complex for a five-year old to understand! When *my* generation, in the chronologically structured history class, some 10 years later finally arrived at Nazi Germany and Second World War, we felt exhausted; hadn't we already discussed the matter sufficiently in the German lessons, social studies, and religion course? It wasn't us, was it? Today, in picking up a current debate, I totally agree when it comes to the question of whether immigrant children should join their indigenous classmates in visiting the concentration camp memorials. Yes, everybody *please* go there! Look at the horror and talk about what happened, to make sure history doesn't repeat itself.

The Two Germanys of 1949–1990 and Beyond

In 1938, German troops occupied Austria ("Anschluss Österreichs ans Reich"), the home country of Adolf Hitler. Next on his agenda was Czechoslovakia, and on September 1, 1939, when German troops seized the Free City of Danzig and entered Poland, the Second World War (1939–1945) began. Depending on where you come from, you must, to a greater or lesser extent, be aware of how people all over the world suffered from this terrible war that Germans were (or are) to blame for.

Germany was defeated, and on the whole, the *Thousand-Year Reich* did not last much longer than 12 years (1933–1945). What was left came under the rule of the four victorious powers—Great Britain, France, the United States, and the Soviet Union. Russia, which in many aspects had suffered *exceptionally* during the Second World War, began to literally dismantle the occupied territory, while the Western Allies soon focused on stabilizing the three Western Zones.

On June 20, 1948, the D-Mark was introduced in the so-called tri-zone that was controlled by the Western powers, and from one day to the next, people saw a great variety of goods displayed in shop windows, including things that were formerly bartered or secretly traded in the black market. The introduction of the new currency and the soon-to-follow "economic miracle" (that was not *so* much of a miracle, as some historians argue, given the extent of the still intact industrial infrastructure) are of great importance for the formation of the (West) German identity; so are the so-called rubble women (*Trümmerfrauen*), who are said to have rebuilt the country with their bare hands. The myth has recently been deconstructed (Treber 2014), however, the icon "Trümmerfrau" will surely last a while longer; people have seen her picture far too often to quickly wipe out the memory.

In 1949, first, the Federal Republic of Germany, and then, the German Democratic Republic (GDR) were founded. In the early 1980s, when my father began to talk to me about democracy, telling me that people in the *other* Germany could not express their opinions freely, I (for some time) believed that *we* lived in the GDR. To say that the German *Democratic* Republic was *not exactly* democratic is an understatement: criticizing their brothers and sisters in the West for re-establishing former Nazis in exalted positions, people in the earlier Soviet Zone soon got used to their own system of aggression and suppression. The State Security Service, Stasi, quickly began to establish an extensive network of informers who were spying on their neighbors, colleagues, and even family members. The *Anti-Fascist Protection Rampart* (the Berlin Wall), thrown up in 1961, was only *one* means of preventing people from leaving the country; gunfire and even tanks were used to suppress people.

Although living in the strongest economy under the Soviet rule, people in socialist East Germany often had to wait for years when they wanted to buy a car or install a telephone connection. Employment was guaranteed in the centrally planned economy, but jobs often did not match peoples' qualifications or talents. Careers greatly depended on whether or not the people (and their relatives) toed the party-line. To criticize the system could easily cost you your place at university.

The GDR film industry and theater scene flourished; however, films, books, music, and other forms of art criticizing the establishment were censored, and artists were often barred from their profession (through political pressure), if not outright incarcerated. The critically acclaimed 2006 drama film, *The Life of Others* (*Das Leben der Anderen*), is said to describe the matter in an exceptionally authentic manner. Another movie dealing with the daily life in East Germany and the crumbling of the Wall that I can recommend is *Good Bye, Lenin!* The 2003 tragicomedy follows a family whose mother is dedicated to the socialist cause and falls into a coma shortly before the 1989 revolution; when she wakes up eight months later, her son attempts to protect her from fatal shock by not telling her about the fall of the Berlin Wall. What I especially like about the movie is the change of perspective: when the two Germanys re-united, it was not seen as a merger among equals. In fact, the East was integrated in the West, and the approximately 16 million people from the East were often (and maybe still sometimes *are*) perceived as being somewhat backward and lazy. Those in the East who had demonstrated against the regime were often accused of only being interested in what the glitzy consumer world in the West had to offer.

Both the separation *and* the reunification of Germany were, for many, a traumatic experience. Quite a few people in the East discovered that their lives were an open book for the Stasi, thanks to their loved ones' surveillance and betrayal. Many lost their jobs with no prospect of ever being employed again. They were humiliated by an attitude and approach that one could easily call colonial. There was an influx of gold diggers from the West, and there were cases wherein the people in the East were outsmarted or even cheated by those more familiar with the capitalist world. People in the East began to call their Western brothers and sisters "*Besserwessis*," a play on a word indicating that those from the West ("*Wessi*") knew everything better. The term "*Ossi*," for those living in the East, had a negative connotation and did not require an extra lexeme to reflect the speaker's dismissive attitude. The pictures of November 9, 1989, when the Wall came down, are iconic; however, there was not much to follow that would emotionally weld the new nation together.

While many countries (can) celebrate the birthday of their nation with great pomp on the anniversary of a revolution or independence from a colonial rule or other occupying forces, Germans, on *their* national day, soberly remember the latest attempt of rather artificial nation-building: On October 3, 1990, the Unification Treaty came into effect and shaped what is now considered "Germany." While other (ex-)world powers indulge in the reminiscences of former glory, Germans are petrified when looking at the glorious mess they have caused in the first half of the 20th century. And, while other nationalities (can) identify with strong heroes like Jeanne d'Arc (Joan of Arc), Wilhelm Tell (William Tell), Mahatma Gandhi, or at least some down-to-earth royal family, contemporary Germans, when asked about identity-establishing personalities, would most probably refer vaguely to Germany as the "land of poets and thinkers." Ironically, the famous writer Johann Wolfgang von Goethe (1749–1832) was not exactly a great fan of the idea of the German nation that had been heavily promoted during his time (Borchmeyer 2017, pp. 44–53).

Giving it more thought, some people might finally mention the former Chancellor, Helmut Kohl (1930–2017), referring to him as the "father of the German reunification." Kohl was in charge when the former occupying countries needed to be convinced that they should grant full sovereignty to a unified German state. However, he was not exactly a charismatic person, and the political and personal scandals uncovered after his chancellorship might be more present in the younger generations' memory than his great achievements in the context of the reunification (and the European Union).

What Germans *were* able to identify with, perhaps to a much greater extent, was the former currency, *Deutsche Mark* (*D-Mark, DM*). Introduced in the tri-zone (what later would become West Germany) in 1948, the money initially stood for the economic miracle; it increasingly became to represent stability, growth, power, and what you could overall call a German success story. Nevertheless, in 1999, the euro was introduced, becoming the currency of more than 300 million people in Europe. At first, an invisible currency only used for accounting purposes, the euro "materialized" in 2002 (European Central Bank n.d.). It replaced, at fixed conversion rates, the banknotes and coins of the national currencies; the pain of separation afflicted many, including business people, who needed to learn to "trust" the new currency. Fears concerning a rather soft currency have proved unfounded. Since the introduction of the euro, we have had a lower inflation rate than under DM times. Nevertheless, the euro has not been able to challenge the U.S. dollar for first place as the world's trading currency.

"Made in Germany" is another idea (icon) people over here generally like(d) to identify with. We will have a look at the history of the slogan and some recent developments in Chapter 3.

CHAPTER 3

What You Should Know About Our Economy

Labor Market and Employment

In 2017, the unemployment rate reached its lowest level in more than 25 years: 5.7 percent (Presse-und Informationsamt der Bundesregierung 2018). I am only partially enthusiastic about these figures, considering certain developments: many people with low incomes are increasingly dependent on transfer payments (e.g., an allowance for rent) to make ends meet. It goes without saying that they cannot save money for their retirement, and with the low payments they will receive from the state pension scheme and due to the fact that most (elderly) people do not live in joint families/with their grown-up children, they are later threatened by poverty in old age (Altersarmut). A recent study by the economic research institutes DIW and ZEW, commissioned by the Bertelsmann Stiftung, shows that, in 2036, one in five 67-year-olds (67 is currently the official retirement age) will be at risk of poverty in old age. According to the authors of the study, the poverty risk of new retirees will rise from 16.2 percent at present to 20.2 percent nationwide (Preker 2017). I will be talking about (the risk of) poverty a bit more later in the text.

The so-called "shortage of skilled workers" (Fachkräftemangel) is a topic controversially discussed in the media; it is not uncommon to suspect that company owners want to depress salaries, asking to (increasingly) recruit employees from abroad. Instead of paying caregivers and nurses properly (no matter where they come from, I might add) and generally improving the working conditions, they want to recruit cheap human resources—for example, from the Eastern European countries, Vietnam, or the Philippines. I am missing a social discourse about the inherent imperialistic viewpoint: instead of exploiting people by subduing foreign countries, nowadays it is better to let them come to our country and exploit them here?

Also, over the past few years, a kind of shadow economy has established itself, in which the long-term unemployed in so-called "1-Euro-Jobs" (EUR 1/hour) are either occupied with pointless, unsatisfactory jobs or work productively for entrepreneurs who are benefitting from the availability of a cheap labor force. The ARD/WDR documentary "Die Armutsindustrie" (The Poverty Industry) shows how grown-ups put together 5,000-piece puzzles, which are to be sold in a store selling used toys; they spend days to see whether maybe one piece was missing after all. The film also shows highly skilled engineers who are manufacturing trampolines, a product that you would normally rather import from China (Die Armutsindustrie 2009). Profiteers of the systems are the institutions that receive funds for "occupying" the unemployed people with nonsense tasks such as aforementioned, or manufacturers and service providers who sell their products and services at competitive prices, which they can afford by paying (state-subsidized) dumping wages to the long-term unemployed. Furthermore, (even) highly qualified (maybe sometimes overqualified) job seekers are often "parked" in "Maßnahmen" (what can be translated to "activities" or "sanctions") of the employment office ("Arbeitsamt" or "Jobcenter," as what we call it now), and are thus not visible in the unemployment statistics. I do not want to say that there is no "war for talent." Many companies often spend months looking for qualified personnel; however, sometimes offering better salaries might help that situation. Anyway, I present no more social criticism at this point.

If you have landed a proper job in Germany, you are in a comparably good situation, I would say. The average full-time weekly working time is around 38 hours; part-time employees work an average of 16.4 hours (Braun and Diekmann 2017). There are extensive occupational health and safety laws (Arbeitsschutzgesetze) that regulate, for example, regular breaks and limit the maximum working time to 10 hours a day (albeit, that would not apply for managerial staff). The fact that these rules are often subverted, especially in connection with the so-called "trust-based working time" (Vertrauensarbeitszeit), is another story. Employees below the age of 18 years enjoy special protection rights, and employers better not violate them.

By law, employees in Germany are entitled to four weeks of vacation per year; *de facto*, most enjoy at least five, if not six weeks. Many companies have a works council (Betriebsrat) that represents employees' interests. There are also regulations on maternity protection (Mutterschutz), parental leave (for mothers *and* fathers), and currently, the right for part-time workers to return to full-time employment is under deliberation.

If an employee survived the probationary period of (usually) six months, he or she can only be dismissed in very special cases; for example, if the company is forced to lay-off personnel due to economic difficulties. But, even then, there is a so-called social plan (Sozialplan), which provides that older employees who have a family should be given preference to stay in the company, rather than young employees without a family, for instance. We do not have a hire-and-fire mentality, like in the United States.

Out of the approximately 44 million people employed in 2017, 1.4 percent were working in the so-called primary sector, that is, in agriculture and forestry, or fishing (Land-und Forstwirtschaft, Fischerei). About 24.1 percent found work in the manufacturing industry (Produzierendes Gewerbe), and with 74.5 percent of all employees working in the service industry and other sectors (Übrige Wirtschaftsbereiche, Dienstleistungen), the tertiary sector has yet again grown (Statistisches Bundesamt 2018a).

According to the Federal Ministry for Economic Affairs and Energy (BMWi), a good 80 percent of all companies in Germany are service companies (Bundesministerium für Wirtschaft und Energie 2018a). The largest service sectors, in terms of the gross value added and share of employed persons, are public services, real estate services, business services, and trade. The service sector accounts for 69 percent of the GDP. The BMWi states that "Der Industriestandort Deutschland ist ohne Dienstleistungen kaum noch denkbar" (Germany as an industrial location is hardly conceivable without services) and emphasizes that the production of goods is increasingly interlinked with services. "Wo ein modernes Industrieprodukt die Produktionsstätte verlässt, hat eine lange Reihe von Dienstleistungen zu seiner Entstehung beigetragen, von der Logistik in der Zulieferung über die mechanische Wartung der Produktionsmittel bis zur Softwareunterstützung" (When a modern industrial product leaves the production site, a long series of services have contributed to its creation, from logistics in the supply chain through mechanical maintenance of the means of production to software support), says the institute (ibid). When the product is then sold to the customer, the BMWi sees significantly more services involved, for example, marketing, financing, logistics, and repair. As the next step, let us focus on the most important industry branches in Germany.

Things We Are (Especially) Good At

Discussing whether the economic miracle of the 1950s really *had* been so much of a "miracle," Werner Abelshauser (2018, p. 8), Professor for Historical Social Sciences at Bielefeld University, argues that, although major cities like Hamburg, Cologne, Frankfurt, and Berlin were bombed to rubble and people were poor, post-war (West) Germany could quickly build on what had been achieved during the second Industrial Revolution (1870–1914). This could be largely because of the practice of setting up factories on the city outskirts (as shown in Chapter 1). So, when the cities were bombed—events that are very present in the collective memory—this did not *greatly* affect the German (arms) industry (ibid.). Exceptions are, for example, the cities of Essen, where Krupp's armaments and ammunitions factories were located, and Ludwigshafen/Mannheim, where you would find BASF (then "IG Farben," who, among other products, had equipped the Nazis with synthetic rubber, gasoline, and the lethal gas Zyklon-B). After the war, a great share of the machinery and manufacturing plants in the Soviet zone was deconstructed and shipped to the Soviet Union; however, people in the West were comparably spared from paying war reparations, and after 1947, the Allied even promoted a quick rebuild of the industry.

While the first Industrial Revolution—which began in Great Britain around 1760—mainly resulted in new manufacturing processes being applied in mechanized factories, the second Industrial Revolution highlighted the fashion in which science and technology cross-fertilized each other and drastically changed people's working and living conditions. In this period, some major game-changing inventions were made that accelerated the technological progress yet again and resulted in increased life expectancy and higher standards of living. The invention of chemical fertilizers, for example, raised agricultural productivity, and better techniques and products were developed to store and preserve food.

Until the mid-19th century, engineering, medical technology, and agriculture were "pragmatic bodies of applied knowledge in which things were known to work, but rarely was it understood why they worked" (Mokyr 1998, p. 1). By contrast, the second Revolution increasingly saw scientists (versus polymath Renaissance men) engaged in finding out *how* things work rather than why. Distinctive disciplines like physics and chemistry, as we know them today, evolved, and people looked for universal laws; newly invented equipment and instruments stimulated the process and supported their work.

The 19th century witnessed quite a few Germans being ahead by a nose when it came to breakthrough discoveries: Justus von Liebig (1803–1873), Robert Bunsen (1811–1899), and Hermann Kolbe (1818–1884), for example, were scientists whose work became the foundation for the soon-to-flourish chemical and medical industries. Werner von Siemens (1816–1892) helped establish an entirely new discipline, namely *Elektrotechnik* (electrical engineering), and Robert Bosch (1861–1942) was yet another engineer and inventor whose name still stands for state-of-the-art machine building and automation (Watson 2010, pp. 355–81).

With the steady accumulation of useful knowledge, the way products were developed changed considerably, as did the organization of the production process: the assembly line was already there, but the advent of technology for the production of interchangeable parts rapidly changed the game and started to replace manual handicraft. Those who managed to produce standardized parts or the tools and machines necessary for their manufacturing were ahead of the others in economies of scale. Over here, the investment banks Deutsche Bank and Dresdner Bank, as well as the German state's interventions played a major role in fueling the progress. Industrialists often collaborated (rather than competed) to implement certain desirable standard procedures and industrial norms (Fulbrook 2004, p. 138).

Today, Germans may not be especially good at, or even interested in, mass production. Rather, they are experts when it comes to building *highly specialized* parts and precision tools, and you'd get in touch with them when you need fully automated machines, production processes, and manufacturing plants engineered. However, machinery currently ranks "only" second (14.4 percent) when looking at the most important export items. Accounting for 18.4 percent, motor vehicles and parts thereof were Germany's main export products in 2017 (Statistisches

Bundesamt 2018f). Rudolf Diesel (1858–1913), Carl Benz (1844–1929), Gottlieb Daimler (1834–1900), and Wilhelm Maybach (1846–1929) even today stand for Germany's most significant industry. The third important export category in 2017, by the way, was chemical products (9.0 percent). You may turn back a few pages and cross-check with Table 1.3 to see the extent to which the aforementioned industries are represented in the top 25 most important SMEs in Germany.[1]

Table 3.1 provides an overview of the export and import volumes in euros as of June 2018 in the above, and some other selected segments

Table 3.1 Exports and imports (special trade) by division of the National Product Classification for Production Statistics 2017 (selected categories)

		In million euros	
Division	**Commodity description**	**Exports**	**Imports**
GP09-01	Products of agriculture and hunting	9,749	31,280
GP09-06	Crude petroleum and natural gas	6,249	56,169
GP09-10	Food products	54,232	46,642
GP09-11	Beverages	5,644	5,883
GP09-13	Textiles	11,697	10,976
GP09-14	Wearing apparel	18,361	32,833
GP09-17	Paper and paper products	19,629	15,053
GP09-19	Coke and refined petroleum products	12,463	20,344
GP09-20	Chemicals and chemical products	115,001	79,107
GP09-21	Basic pharmaceutical products and pharmaceutical preparations	76,007	53,986
GP09-22	Rubber and plastic products	46,025	30,706
GP09-23	Other non-metallic mineral products	15,487	11,078
GP09-24	Basic metals	54,250	58,968
GP09-25	Fabricated metal products, except machinery and equipment	43,664	29,373
GP09-26	Computer, electronic, and optical products	111,081	113,253
GP09-27	Electrical equipment	83,373	60,560
GP09-28	Machinery and equipment n.e.c.	184,606	81,329
GP09-29	Motor vehicles, trailers, and semi-trailers	234,811	115,434
GP09-30	Other transport equipment	58,118	32,780

[1] As per *Die Deutsche Wirtschaft*

(Statistisches Bundesamt 2018g). In 2017, the People's Republic of China was Germany's most important trading partner for the second consecutive year. Next came the Netherlands, followed by the United States. In the same year, France dropped from second to fourth on the list; from 1975 to 2014, France had been Germany's most important trading partner.

Talents We Might Lack

Talking about trade, what shortcomings could you experience when dealing with Germans? As we have looked at discoveries and inventions, the slogan "Customer is King" most probably *wasn't* coined by a German. In service-wasteland Germany, people are fairly used to what *you* could easily perceive as impoliteness. Over here, some might even become wary or suspicious if someone was *too* nice and friendly. Many would prefer a genuinely grumpy (but competent) account representative over someone who just *pretends* to enjoy serving them. Plus, in a country where expertise is held in high regard and companies invest heavily in the education of their youngsters, the customer *cannot* always be right *per se*, right? That would make the staff look stupid, wouldn't it?

Travel Writer Cal O Cal, coming from the United States, is used to a "Customer first" attitude from pretty much any business; what people understand by customer service here and there, however, differs. "Germany's still got a bit of ground to cover in this regard," he opines. "Although it is changing very rapidly, most Germans think it is quite normal *not* to put the customer first." O Cal also finds it hard to digest how you "still need to send a written snail-mail letter to cancel any service," which, he thinks, is outdated. "If I am in a Telekom service center, standing in front a representative who is looking at my account, after verifying who I am, why he cannot simply cancel a service I no longer need is beyond me," he says, comparing German business practices with the United States, "where pretty much anything is possible via a toll-free phone call." I can truly empathize with O Cal; however (and because it is high time a German high-school graduate worth his or her salt did so), let me take the opportunity to quote from Goethe's Faust (First Part):

> *Denn, was man schwarz auf weiß besitzt,*
> *Kann man getrost nach Hause tragen.*
>
> *what one has down in black and white*
> *one can carry home contentedly.*
>
> *(von Goethe 2007, pp. 152, 153)*

Nevertheless, just like I do *not* believe that every German is a great poet or thinker, it would never occur to me to argue that people over here are all gifted engineers and great inventors; although, I *do* observe certain traits, customs, and behaviors that *somehow* seem to be connected with how particular industries prosper. Even at the risk of being accused of stereotyping, I would suggest that Germans overall are more concerned about precision than people from many other countries. Not only do we expect that a screw should *precisely*, rather than somewhat, fit the wall plug, we also greatly value precise instructions and clear communication. Be careful when using the word "pragmatic" in a business conversation because some consider pragmatism the source of all evil. As thoroughly thought through, long-term solutions are generally preferred over quick fixes, the entrepreneurs' and industrialists' planning horizons might be much longer here than in other parts of the world, like in the United States, for example. Workers' participation can sometimes slow things down further, especially when the employee representatives fear changes for the worse!

Over here, people are less inclined toward taking risks, and to some extent, prefer to build on technologies with a certain degree of maturity. However, that is not the best possible breeding ground for innovations in advanced technologies such as IT, semiconductors, or biotechnology (Abelshauser 2012, p. 48). I would suggest that Germany is also not the first place you should come to when you are looking for venture capital. What *can* indeed promote innovation are the regional clusters, as introduced in Chapter 1.

"Made in Germany" and the Dual Education System

For many people all over the world, "Made in Germany" stands for high efficiency work leading to safe, precision-made, high-tech, reliable, and long-lasting, but also expensive and not-always-customer-focused products. "Perfection to the last detail," like Osman Bayazit Genc, a general manager in the tourism industry from Turkey put it. Perfectionism, if you can afford it money- and time-wise, is one thing, but sometimes, products and services can just get totally over-engineered. My favorite example of this phenomenon are the huge and robust Deutsche Bahn ticket vending machines with their big touchscreen monitors; when you have managed to complete the complicated order process (*phew!*), better collect *all* the receipts that are slowly printed one after another, so as to make sure you do not leave the actual ticket behind!

We owe the slogan to the British who, at the end of the 19th century, forced foreign producers to label their products with the country of origin. The idea was to make the Brits "buy British." The campaign backfired and the label "Made in Germany" ultimately developed into a sign of superior quality (Deutsche Welle 2012). Many also associate this tagline with loyalty and trustworthiness, although we will see how the recent scandals involving major players in the banking and automotive industries—the Diesel emissions scandal, including unethical emissions tests—will harm the "hitherto good" (some might also say: sometimes overrated) image of German products in the long run.

How come German products are (overall) of superior quality? In task-oriented Germany, expertise is greatly valued, and many, without even reflecting on it, strive for (or suffer from) perfectionism. When you deal with a German, expect to be speaking to an expert in his or her field. According to the data published by the Federal Employment Agency (Bundesagentur für Arbeit 2018a) as of September 2017, about 62 percent of all people in an employment relationship subject to social insurance contribution[2] had a professional qualification (mit anerkanntem Berufsabschluss) and approximately 16 percent were academics (mit akademischem Berufsabschluss).

And, how do people typically become experts in their fields? A very common start to a German's career path, especially when you like to work

---

[2] That would *not* include the so-called Mini-Jobs with a (for now) maximum salary of 450 euros per month. Social insurance contributions can include, for example, mandatory payments for unemployment insurance, pension insurance, and health insurance.

in trade, is to undertake a dual vocational education and training (Duale Berufsausbildung). Depending on the recognized trade you want to pursue (anerkannter Ausbildungsberuf), the standard training duration is two to three years. Currently, you can choose between 326 trades (Statista GmbH 2018a), such as Shop Assistant (Verkäufer/-in), Management Assistant in Wholesale and Foreign Trade (Kaufmann/-frau für Groß- und Außenhandel), Metal Cutting Mechanic (Zerspanungsmechaniker/-in), Alterations Tailor (Änderungsschneider/-in), or Plant Mechanic for HVAC and Sanitary Engineering (Anlagenmechaniker/-in für Sanitär-, Heizungs- und Klimatechnik). In some trades, trainees also need to choose between various specializations (e.g., the aforementioned mechanic would need to pursue a career in air-conditioning, heating, or renewable energies).

The minimum entry qualification for any apprenticeship is the degree that you get when you have successfully completed nine years of schooling at a so-called Mittelschule (which could be translated as middle school). For some trades, employers prefer to hire teenagers who completed 10 years of schooling, and in some cases, even Abitur (which you can reach after 12–13 years of schooling at a secondary school) is the required entry ticket for pursuing your dream job. Depending on which of the 16 federal states you live in, school attendance is compulsory for up to 12 years (including trade school as described next) (Bax n.d.). The literacy rate in Germany is commonly said to have been 99 percent for years; however, a study conducted by the University of Hamburg in 2011 claimed that around 7.5 million people in Germany could not read and write properly (they are considered functional illiterates), while 2.3 million people between the ages of 18 and 64 years were completely illiterate. According to the university's findings, they can write their names and individual words, but can neither read nor understand whole sentences (Bundesministerium für Bildung und Forschung n.d.).

Every company that takes on trainees needs to appoint at least one certified in-house education officer/mentor (Ausbildungsbeauftragte/-r) who is not only a subject-matter expert, but is also pedagogically trained and well-versed with the German Youth Employment Protection Act. This person needs to ensure that the training is organized in accordance with the criteria catalog of the Chamber of Industry and Commerce (there is one catalog for each of the specific trades), and that, for the theoretical part of the education, the trainees (Auszubildende, short: Azubis) are enrolled at the nearest trade school (Berufsschule) that offers specialized programs for the specific trade. I, for example, spent about 12 weeks a year at a trade school in Nuremberg. The final exams consisted of a highly standardized written test (multiple-choice questions) and a colloquium conducted by, if I remember correctly, two industry experts and one representative of the Chamber. The committee also went through the record book that I, like every apprentice in Germany, had to maintain for the duration of my apprenticeship. Trainees need to follow the daily protocol of noting down what they have done on each day of their apprenticeship.

If you want to launch a business, for many professions, a so-called Master Craftsman or Master Tradesman Certificate (Meisterbrief) is mandatory (Bundesministerium für Wirtschaft und Energie 2018b). For example, pastry chefs, butchers, and carpenters need to enroll in one of the more than 3,000 German master schools, where they are to enhance their theoretical and practical knowledge and also need to attend courses in business administration, law, and teaching methods and theory (so that they can train apprentices). The cost for such schooling varies from 4,000 to 9,000 euros (depending on the craft or trade) and on top of additional expenses like travel costs, about 750 euros are to be borne for examination fees as well. The pay-off can normally be enjoyed after four or five years (Deutsche Handwerks Zeitung 2016). I doff my hat to my hairdresser who invested this kind of time and money to be allowed to operate her salon. I have followed her career and enjoyed her craftsmanship for some 15 years now.

Generally speaking, Germans are loyal, think long term, and like to build things that last. Especially in Western Germany, people are not terribly interested in quick fixes (nor are they good at improvising). If you are inclined to make temporary arrangements, your patchwork fixes could be frowned upon and even considered illegal. I remember how I, during the winter (!), stopped using the instant boiler in my apartment in Delhi, "although" it had been fixed with tape and strings three times; in Germany, the bathroom area could easily have been locked down for security reasons. If you want to connect a lamp or replace an outlet, you are supposed to hire an electrician. However, please free to change a faulty light bulb yourself.

The Relevance of Chambers and Trade Associations

Even if sometimes rather unapproachable when expected to socialize in a somewhat personal context, Germans like to mix and mingle professionally. When it is to their advantage or it serves a larger cause, managers and company owners are often ready to cooperate with businesses that are in the same industry, sometimes even with their competitors (Abelshauser 2012, pp. 38–41). I am not talking about cartels and price rigging—which I do not deny may exist—but about a great variety of trade associations and initiatives. The *Verband Deutscher Maschinen- und Anlagenbau* (VDMA), for example, represents more than 3,200 member companies in the mechanical and systems engineering industry in Germany and Europe, mainly looking at common economic, technological, and scientific interests (VDMA e.V. – Mechanical Engineering Industry Association n.d.). When I last accessed their website, the landing page of the German Association of the Automotive Industry (VDA) read "*Quo vadis, Diesel?*"[3] The VDA currently represents more than 600 companies that manufacture cars, trailers, bodies, and buses, as well as parts and accessories; and, it is concerned with more than just the question of how the recent diesel emission scandal will affect the industry in the long run (Verband der Automobilindustrie e.V. (VDA) 2018). One of their major activities is the staging of the IAA trade shows. There is even an association for enterprise federations, industry working groups, and industry-affiliated service providers, which is the *Bundesverband der Deutschen Industrie e.V.* (BDI). The Federation of German Industries focuses "the joint interests of its member associations and represent[s] these in dealings with parliament and society." The BDI "represents the interests of 100,000 businesses with eight million employees" (Bundesverband der Deutschen Industrie e.V. (BDI) n.d.).

But, there are *many* more smaller and often very specialized associations. Just yesterday—during a dedicated networking event—did I speak

---

[3] "Quo vadis?" is Latin and can be translated as "Where are you going?" The ancient language is (still) taught in some German Gymnasien (high schools); with 42.4 percent of high-school pupils learning Latin, the share—according to data published in 2014—is especially high in Bavaria, while students in Bremen (13.8) and the Saarland (11.2) rarely study the dead language (Bolz 2014).

to representatives of several associations that especially represent women in business: (young) professionals, entrepreneurs, company owners, and so on. *deutscher ingenieurinnenbund e. V.* (an association for female engineers) was there, *FidAR : Frauen in die Aufsichtsräte e. V.*, an association promoting the increase of the women's share on the supervisory boards was there, but I think I haven't seen anybody from *BLV : Ladies in Logistics.*

As you can see, personal relationships may become less relevant when you are embedded in a quite easily accessible and tightly institutionalized network that you can rely upon; and even you can tap these networks and try to make use of their resources! Some associations, like the Association of German Engineers (VDI), explicitly seek and maintain close relationships with an international audience (VDI Verein Deutscher Ingenieure e.V. n.d.). The network of the German Chambers of Commerce Abroad (AHKs) consists of bilateral chambers of commerce abroad. They consult and represent German companies worldwide that wish to develop or expand their business activities in the respective countries (Deutscher Industrie- und Handelskammertag (DIHK) e.V. n.d.). I suggest you get in touch with your local chamber and find out whether you can participate in conferences or networking events that target German business people wanting to do business in your country.

Associations are also always a good starting point when you need to learn about certain industry standards that are (maybe) relevant for exporting your products to Germany. If you want to sell electronic goods, for example, the Waste Electrical and Electronic Equipment Directive (WEEE) or Restriction of Hazardous Substances Directive (RoHS) are matters you need to get acquainted with. For that purpose, I suggest you first try to get in touch with ZVEI, the German Electrical and Electronic Manufacturers' Association. On their website, they inform about economic policies, business cycles and markets, and so on (Zentralverband Elektrotechnik- und Elektronikindustrie e.V. n.d.).

And, how would you identify the associations relevant for you? Either you go through the BDI's website (https://english.bdi.eu/bdi/members/) or you check out who are the media partners of relevant trade fairs (more on that topic in Chapter 6). Very often, the events are supported, if not organized, by the relevant associations. Or, simply try a keyword search: "my industry" plus "association" or (in German) "Verband."

How We (Like to) Spend Our Money

Since you are reading this text, I assume that, at some point, you plan to sell to or buy from Germany. Therefore, you should be interested in understanding how people generally (like to) spend their money and what they spend it on. In case you are targeting private consumers, you also need to know what their average disposable incomes are.

First of all, remember that whatever product or service you are trying to offer, chances are high that it is already here; Germany is a highly developed B2B market. Try to imagine why people would be unhappy with the existing offer, who may or may not yet have access to this kind of offer, and who may be unhappy with their current suppliers. If you're adding a special feature or an enhanced service to a standard product (as applicable in your country), to what extent would that extra be appreciated in Germany? Is the infrastructure similar to what you might find in your own country? If, for example, you look at payment methods or Internet coverage, Germany might, in some respects, be less developed than other European countries. Trying to answer these questions can help you get a clue about whom to approach in the first place. We'll discuss the what, why, and how at greater length later in the book (Chapter 6).

Some of the things that you should keep in mind when you want business people to spend money on your products or services are that, first of all, Germans are generally much less risk-inclined than people from many other cultures. Their understanding of the word "risk" may vary considerably from how you and your colleagues would define the term. While you might think that they want to bargain over the price, your German counterparts might be hesitant to close the deal over imponderables not yet sufficiently addressed in the (selling) process. They would very often want to consider and discuss the long-term implications of an investment with you, their team, their superiors, their lawyers, and so on; this takes time.

When you buy from them, things may (also) not always be smooth sailing, especially if they have had not-so-pleasant experiences with similar buyers (or perhaps even you) in the past. If you are from a country that does not rank especially high when it comes to political and economic stability, you should think about how you can make your sellers feel comfortable that they will, sooner or later, receive their money, preferably in euros or maybe U.S. dollars. When talking about trust-building initiatives, I am not (only) referring to trying to socialize with them; Germans rely on personal networks much less than people in most other countries of the world. They would much rather rely on iron-clad contracts and law-enforcing institutions. When they feel that people are talking about monkey business (assessing the behavior or situation from *their* perspective and cultural background), they might even drop the discussions at a very early stage. When I worked in electronics components distribution, we would not even discuss quotations with (former) customers with pending dues or people who, in our perception, were trying to bargain like stall owners at a bazaar; and even when you are ready to spend big money, be careful not to assume that people wouldn't be interested in how you are using their products. If it is in conflict with their personal values (in case of smaller businesses) or code of conduct (for bigger firms), sellers might refuse to cater to your needs.

Speaking of B2C, in most cases, you would look at Germans as customers. With a gross domestic product (GDP) per capita of 45,229.25 U.S. dollars in 2017 (adjusted by purchasing power parity (PPP)), Germany can certainly be considered one of the richer countries in the world. Looking at the current G20 countries, only Switzerland, the United States, and the Netherlands rank higher. However, looking at Europe, the German GDP per capita ranks a mere 10th, and that is behind countries like Sweden, Denmark, Norway, and Austria. On an international level, the roughly 45,000 U.S. dollars is equivalent to 255 percent of the world's average (TRADING ECONOMICS n.d.). If you would like to quickly look up your own country's GDP and rank, I suggest you refer to www.tradingeconomics.com.

When researching the *average* disposable income of people over here, there are some points to be considered. I have already mentioned the fact that the gap between the rich and poor has widened considerably over the past years (some would say decades). According to the Federal Statistical Office (Destatis), in 2016, the average share of people at risk of poverty or social exclusion amounted to 19.7 percent, as compared to 23.5 percent in the European Union (Statistisches Bundesamt 2017). "People are considered to be at risk of poverty or social exclusion if at least one of the following three living conditions applies," Destatis writes: "Their income is below the at-risk-of-poverty threshold" (that is less than 60 percent of the median income of the entire population (Bundeszentrale für politische Bildung 2018)), "the household they live in is severely materially deprived, or the household has a very low work intensity" (Statistisches Bundesamt 2017). According to the EU definition, in Germany, persons living alone currently are at risk of poverty if they have less than 13,152 euros per year, that is 1,096 euros per month, to live on (Europäische Kommission 2018). Destatis explains that payment of public transfer payments considerably reduces the at-risk-of-poverty rate of the population: In Germany, the at-risk-of-poverty rate *before* social transfers (except pension payments) in 2014 amounted to 25 percent (Statistisches Bundesamt 2015). One flaw of the method of calculation is: even students who live on their own and receive generous support from their parents can fall under the risk of poverty category (Cremer 2016, pp. 47–50).

The (only recently introduced) mandatory minimum wage is currently 8.84 euros per hour (Deutsche Welle 2018), that is, looking at a standard work week, around 1,500 euros per month. There are some exceptions—for example, for certain kinds of internships or if people are hired after long-term unemployment. The numbers certainly do not apply to freelancers and self-employed people. The minimum wage mostly applies for jobs done by less-qualified employees. Looking at the other end of the spectrum, according to career service Absolventa, the average salary of "vollzeitbeschäftigte Fach- und Führungskräfte" (full-time working specialists and executive staff) in 2017 was 4,846 euros, that is, an annual income of about 58,152 euros (Absolventa GmbH 2018).

Let us take a look at the average income per household and understand what to consider when making calculations and projections. In 2016, the average household income was 4,337 euros per month (4,555 euros in the former Federal Republic of Germany without Berlin, and 3,515 euros in the new Länder). Broken down into income sources, on an average, 2,718 euros were generated by employment, 33 euros by self-employment, and 961 euros by public transfer payments. On an average 421 euros were generated from assets, which, for sure, would only apply to the smaller share of all households, while 205 euros came from nonpublic transfer payments—that could, for example, be continued paying of remuneration in the event of illness—and income from subleasing (Statistisches Bundesamt n.d.). Remember, we are still talking about *gross* income! To arrive at the disposable income, we need to deduct social insurance contributions. On an average, that would be 583 euros for unemployment insurance, pension insurance, health insurance, and so on. We also need to subtract income or wage tax and the so-called "Solidaritätszuschlag" (solidarity surcharge)—a special tax that has been introduced in the 1990s to, among other things, finance the reunification of Germany (Djahangard 2018); added up, that are, at an average 475 euros. The average *net* income per household in the period under review was 3,314 euros, of which 2,480 euros would be spent on private consumption (ibid.).

The aforementioned numbers are maybe quite abstract; so, let us look at some typical incomes: a single person (e.g., a shop assistant) without children and a monthly salary of 1,900 euros (Bundesagentur für Arbeit 2018b) would arrive at a net payment of 1,334 euros (Jobware GmbH 2018). If he or she has to pay church taxes, another 13–15 euros would be deducted, the exact amount depending on which federal state our shop assistant lives in. I mention this so that, in case you have skipped the chapter about regional peculiarities, you might consider going back to it some time (Chapter 1). You can use online salary calculators that are offered by some job portals and insurance companies to do more sample calculations. Keep in mind that the percentage of income tax is progressive (currently ranking from 14 to 42 percent; 45 percent for top earners), and that deductions also depend on whether people are married and / or have kids. People with less than 8,820 euros of taxable income per year—that is, basically, salary minus tax-deductible expenses such as costs for commuting to the workplace—pay no income tax at all (Bundesministerium der Finanzen 2018). A person with the average income of a specialist or executive staff (4,846 euros) would get about 3,200 euros credited to his or her account, provided he or she is married, has two children, and has opted for the most common tax class sparing the higher income in the household (tax category III) (Jobware GmbH 2018).

On an average, a German household spends about one-third of its disposal income on housing, energy, and maintenance of the dwelling; that was 877 euros per month in 2016. About 14 percent was spent on food, beverages, and tobacco, and about the same amount (335 euros) went on transport. The average household would spend about 10 percent on recreation and culture, while budgeting 108 euros per month for clothing and footwear. At first glance, the 18 euros in Table 3.2 (Statistisches Bundesamt 2018c) for education might look odd, but knowing that education is basically free in Germany, the numbers start to make sense.

Those numbers alone are, yet again, just a starting point for your sales activities. You still need to define segments and research your target groups very carefully. A single person in an expensive city like Munich might need to spend up to some 40 percent of his or her disposable income on accommodation—on an average, single households in 2017 had to allocate 31 percent on gross cold lease[4] (Ebert, et al. n.d.)—, while a couple living in the small city of Görlitz, at the Polish border, might only need to allocate some 250 or 300 euros for rent (Immowelt AG 2018); although, living in the place with the lowest average salaries in Germany

Table 3.2 Private consumption expenditure of households[5]

Expenditure 2016: average per household and month	Euros	%
Private consumption expenditure	2,480	100
Food, beverages, and tobacco	342	13.8
Clothing and footwear	108	4.4
Housing, energy, maintenance of the dwelling	877	35.3
Furnishings, equipment, and household maintenance	150	6.1
Health	99	4.0
Transport	335	13.5
Postal communication and telecommunication	62	2.5
Recreation and culture	258	10.4
Education	18	0.7
Restaurants and hotels	142	5.7
Miscellaneous goods and services	90	3.6

[4] Rent, including service charges related to, for example, garbage collection and caretaking, but excluding the cost for heating, warm water, and electricity.

[5] Excluding households of farmers and self-employed persons, as well as households with a monthly net household income of 18,000 euros or over.

(Schubert 2018), one may more easily afford buying a car—an item the city-dweller might not even wish to possess considering the rare and expensive parking spaces and air pollution, or the recently emerged threat/reality of "Diesel-Fahrverbot" (driving bans on diesel-powered vehicles) in Frankfurt, Berlin, Hamburg, Stuttgart, and so on (ADAC e.V. 2018).

As compared to the Swedes or people in Greece, for example, Germans spend less money on food (Statistisches Bundesamt 2018e). The reason can be differing price levels or consumer preferences. If you are French, for example, do not suppose that the average German would value wining and dining as much as the average Frenchman and would spend as much money on gourmet food. While someone with a low income who needs to feed a family would most likely be happy to buy industrially produced and processed milk at 60 eurocents—no matter *how* concerned Germans are overall with nature protection and animal welfare—I have decided that I can still afford to spend 1.49 euros for a liter of milk that is supposedly produced by cows that are kept under comparably good living conditions. However, it would never occur to me to spend hundreds of euros for a (status symbol) coffeemaker or even a cent, let alone 1.50 euros for some artificial, sugary energy drink that comes in a small tin.

CHAPTER 4

What (Else) Makes People in Germany Tick?

What We Vote for (in Life): Current Issues in Politics

Every four years, Germans are called upon to cast their votes in the federal elections (Bundestagswahl). In 2017, 76.2 percent of all eligible voters (i.e., German nationals above the age of 18 years) answered that call (ARD-aktuell/tagesschau.de 2017). However, it took almost half a year (!) until a new government was formed.

So far, in reunited Germany, it has not happened yet that one party has won the majority of seats in the elections for parliament (Bundestag); therefore, it is a standard procedure that the strongest party invites other parties to discuss forming a coalition. Looking at the election outcomes since 1949 (in West Germany), the conservative Christian Democrats (CDU), along with their Bavarian counterpart (sister party), the CSU, in most cases had the upper hand; since 2005, under Chancellor Angela Merkel—a doctor of physics and child to a protestant priest and a schoolteacher who, shortly after their daughter's birth in 1954, moved from Hamburg to the German Democratic Republic. From 2005 to 2009, and yet again from 2013 to 2017, an alliance between the CDU/CSU and the center-left Social Democratic Party (SPD) held office. The years 2009–2013 saw a coalition between CDU/CSU and the Free Democratic Party (FDP).

In September 2017, the CDU/CSU again won the most votes (32.9 percent, as compared with 41.5 percent in the previous elections); this time, however, only minutes after the (preliminary) election result was broadcast, the SPD candidate for the German chancellorship, shooting star Martin Schulz, a bookseller and former President of the European Parliament, categorically ruled out being part of a grand coalition with the CDU/CSU. Although both parties had lost considerable electoral approval (SPD only gained 20.5 percent as compared to 25.7 percent in 2013), gaining the majority of the seats in parliament should have been plain sailing for another grand coalition. A majority in parliament is required to pass legislation.

What followed were weeks-long exploratory talks between the CDU/CSU, the liberal FDP (10.7 percent), and the Greens (Bündnis 90 / Die Grünen: 8.9 percent) to form what the media, referring to the party colors of black, yellow, and green, called the "Jamaica-coalition;" discussions that the FDP leader, Christian Lindner, finally, and quite abruptly, broke off. As the SPD kept insisting on being the strongest power in the opposition, for some time, it seemed likely that the Germans would be called back to the polls; something that Merkel and other high-ranking politicians wanted to avoid at all costs. As far as I remember, only a few representatives of the democratic socialist party, the Die Linke (9.2 percent), for a short while, publicly argued in favor of new elections.

Another option, not exactly seriously considered, was that a minority government could be formed. A setting in which the government needs to form many small issue-based coalitions to pass legislation (a common practice in Denmark, for example) is, with minor exceptions in local politics, a constellation yet unseen in Germany. Merkel and senior members of her party argued that a minority government would be too unstable, slowing the country's ability to pass legislation. Another concern many people articulated was that reaching out to different parties on different issues could also lead to teaming up with the right-wing populist Alternative für Deutschland (AfD), which had entered the Bundestag (with 12.6 percent) only four years after the founding of the party in 2013 (Bleiker 2017).

President Frank-Walter Steinmeier repeatedly spoke to the parties who had surpassed the 5 percent threshold to enter the parliament (as aforementioned) and appealed to them to reconsider their positions. Finally, the SPD agreed to consider dropping their idea of forming an opposition and discussed with their members the pros and cons of forming/being part of a coalition government instead. Only after a member survey, in which 66 percent of the elective 463,723 comrades voted for an alliance with the CDU/CSU, was the formation of a grand coalition finally announced in March 2018 (Albrecht 2018).

What do the aforementioned parties stand for, and how are their positions even similar when it comes to topics they find especially important? A team from the public broadcaster Bayerischer Rundfunk used a learning algorithm to analyze the election programs of the major parties, published in advance of the September 2017 elections. Using machine learning, the team automatically evaluated 810 sections of text and sorted them into categories; this allowed them to juxtapose and compare the parties' positions, arriving, among others, at the following conclusions (Kühne, Schnuck, and Schöffel 2017).

All perused parties attached the greatest importance to welfare and quality of life. This included, for example, statements on the welfare state, environmental protection, (gender) equality, and promotion of culture (funding for theaters, museums, libraries, and so on). The headline of the CDU/CSU's party program spelled that out as "Für ein Deutschland, in dem wir gut und gerne leben" (For a Germany in which we live well and with pleasure). The FDP, calling for new/fresh thinking (Denken wir neu!) attached above-average importance to statements on the economy, while the SPD, who had headlined their political governance program "Zeit für mehr Gerechtigkeit" (it's time for more justice), put extraordinary emphasis on external relations.

The broadcast team analyzed the three most frequently addressed topics for each party; it did not come as a surprise that the Greens, appealing to Germans to more courageously shape their future ("Zukunft wird aus Mut gemacht" / "The future is made out of courage"), attached great importance to environmental protection, while the SPD, the Die Linke ("Die Zukunft, für die wir kämpfen" / "The future we fight for") and the AfD ("Programm für Deutschland" / "Program for Germany") very often addressed social issues. In addition to its traditional topics of freedom and civil rights, the FDP focused on investment in education. The CDU/CSU government program, in many passages, addressed questions of infrastructure and technology, including statements on digitization. All parties argued in favor of increasing pensions and promoting education and culture.

The three most frequently addressed topics of each party have been:

- CDU/CSU: Infrastructure and technology, expansion of the welfare state, and expansion of international relations

- SPD: Social justice, importance of welfare (upgrade), and infrastructure and technology
- Die Linke: Social justice, importance of welfare (upgrade), and environmental protection
- Bündnis 90 / Die Grünen: Environmental protection, social justice, and freedom and civil rights
- FDP: Freedom and civil rights, investment in education, and social justice
- AfD: Importance of welfare (upgrade), social justice, and freedom and civil rights

The Greens and the AfD, in the aforementioned analysis, were found to be on the far right; the latter called for a guiding German culture (Leitkultur), a limitation of immigration, and a repeal of the climate protection plan. The fact that (in this analysis) the Greens also tended to move to the right, compared to other parties, was attributed, for example, to the demands for a child and family-friendly policy; positions that political science tends to assign to a conservative policy line. When the Greens talk about family, however, they do not necessarily mean a traditional constellation (opposite-sex married couple with a child/children), but would also consider "Patchworkfamilien" (blended families), and so on. The Die Linke speaks more boldly in favor of more investment in education and social security systems than other parties, thus positioning itself even a bit further to the left.

The Bayerischer Rundfunk found the positions in the political field of economics also lying closely together. The CDU/CSU, the FDP, and the AfD were all calling for a balanced state budget. The SPD committed to maintaining Germany as an industrial location and highlighted the importance of small and medium-sized businesses. The Die Linke often made classic left-wing statements about the regulation of the financial markets or a halt to privatization.

The most striking differences could be observed in external relations politics. For example, the Die Linke and the Greens argued clearly in favor of disarmament and peace policy; these issues were not quite as important for the SPD, even though they also made demands for disarmament. At the same time, the SPD wanted to modernize the armed forces (Bundeswehr). The CDU/CSU and the FDP were also in favor of more investment in defense. The AfD even wanted to reintroduce compulsory military service, which was suspended in 2011, and to fundamentally reform the Bundeswehr.

What I remember most vividly are the (ongoing) discussions about the social texture (Gesellschaftsgefüge). Security and the fight against crime played a major role in the election programs; however, the perspectives greatly varied: The Die Linke showed itself especially concerned about right-wing violence, while the AfD explicitly regarded, and still regards, violence by foreigners against Germans as a problem.

What I am now observing, and this is one year after the elections, is the harsh tone of voice that has taken hold in the Bundestag, especially when it comes to the "refugee issue," or "refugee crisis," as the influx of migrants that currently dominates the political and social debate, often is referred to.

Now that we have talked about what the Germans worry about (as reflected) in politics, let us take a closer look at what concerns the "average citizen" on a more individual level.

What We (Like to) Take for Granted: Security, Structures, and Status

Some years ago, while doing research for my master's thesis on intercultural children's and young adult literature in Germany, I came across Rena Dumont's autobiographic novel *Paradiessucher* (Paradise Seekers). A writer, filmmaker, and actress living and working in Munich, Dumont was born in (former) Czechoslovakia. In 1986, when she was 17 years old, she and her mother fled to Germany, the supposed paradise. What I found exceptional about the book, apart from the gripping story and her unique style of writing, was the unparalleled way in which Germany is described—from a (former) "outsider's" perspective. For example, on the occasion of visiting a boyfriend's family in a small town in Bavaria:

> *Da ich ausschließlich mit dem Auge wahrnehme, offenbaren sich mir die Gewohnheiten, Launen, Rituale und Sitten unserer Gastgeber*

> *wie von selbst. Es ist interessant zu beobachten. Vielleicht liegt das gerade an der Sprachbarriere. Wortspiele, Phrasen und Papierkorbsätze vernebeln nicht meinen Geist. Ein Spürhund bin ich, der die Außenwelt aus einer anderen Perspektive betrachtet. Kleinbürgertum, Spießigkeit, Selbstgerechtigkeit treten deutlich zutage. (Dumont 2013, p. 156)*
>
> *(Since I perceive exclusively with the eye, the habits, moods, rituals, and customs of our hosts reveal themselves to me seemingly involuntarily. It is interesting to observe. Perhaps this is due to the language barrier. Wordplays, phrases, and wastepaper basket sentences do not cloud my mind. I am a sniffer dog who looks at the outside world from a different perspective. Petty bourgeoisie, philistinism, and self-righteousness clearly come to light.)*

Why do I tell you about the novel when it is not (at least, not yet) available in English? In my opinion, one of the best ways to learn about your own country (and culture) is to discover the view(s) from outside and contemplate the (similarities and) contrasting perspectives. Dumont, through the novel's heroine Lenka, does that too: "Diese Eigenschaften," the book continues, "sind mir nicht unbekannt, weiß Gott, davon kann ich ein Lied singen. Allerdings sind die Tschechen gemäßigte Betonköpfe" (these qualities are not unknown to me. God knows I can sing a song about them. However, the Czechs are moderate dinosaurs / reactionary die-hards). And, off she goes, listing some (not-so-pleasant) character traits she sees in her (former) countrymen (ibid. pp. 256–57).

Collecting ideas and material for this book, I thought it would be nice to also include some "outsiders'" perspectives and stories. To find out what others find typical (or exceptional) about Germany, I asked people in my network—that is, mostly international business people or Germans who travel frequently or have been working abroad for at least some time—questions like "How can you make a German happy?" or "What do you struggle with when it comes to what Germans think is normal?" The answers were overall very much in line with what I had expected (e.g., hinting at certain cultural dimensions or cultural standards that have been discussed extensively in other works[1]); however, some aspects of (mainstream) Germans' "code of conduct" for me now appear in new, or at least clearer, light.

This is how Dumont answered my question on how to make a German/Germans happy: "Du gibst ihnen Sicherheit und Ansehen. Und ein tolles Auto" (you give them security and prestige. And, a great car). In saying this, Dumont touched upon several concepts that are (generally) very important to the (average) German: risk-aversity and the avoidance of uncertainty; a certain preference for hierarchical structures, status, and depending on one's personality, maybe also "being higher up in the pecking order;" and the desire to possess (material) things.

"Schaffe, schaffe, Häusle baue" is a saying that originates from the south of Germany, and as a demand or appeal, describes an attitude to work hard, and even harder, to build (or buy) something; in this common phrase, a wee house. In front of the small house, which is ideally surrounded by a neatly mowed lawn (and maybe decorated with some garden gnomes), and obviously, a fence, you can park your fancy, polished-to-a-shine car—"der Deutschen liebstes Kind" (the Germans' dearest child), as yet another saying goes. I spent my childhood in the countryside, and there at least, that was the case in the 1980s...the buying of new cars was closely monitored in the neighborhood: If the Müllers bought a new car, the Meiers down the road would gossip about how Mr. Müller (!) could afford it, while the Müllers' neighbors, living in the adjoining house on the other side of the fence, would feel growing pressure to soon upgrade their fleet as well.

Political scientist Herfried Münkler, in his book *Die Deutschen und ihre Mythen*, argues that in post-war (West) Germany, "verlagerte sich

---

[1] I do not go into explaining the cultural dimensions as described by Geert Hofstede, Fons Trompenaars, or Edward Hall. For those interested in learning about dimensions of (national) culture, I recommend reading the book *Cultures and Organizations—Software of the Mind: Intercultural Cooperation and Its Importance for Survival* (Hofstede, Hofstede, and Minkov 2010) as introductory literature. With *Doing Business with Germans. Their Perception, Our Perception*, Sylvia Schroll-Machl has published an extensive and highly recommendable treatise on German cultural standards (Schroll-Machl 2008).

das Bedürfnis nach mythischer Narration und symbolischer Repräsentation von Politik und Staat auf Markt und Konsum" (the need for mythical narration and symbolic representation of politics and state shifted to market and consumption). Münkler, in writing about the Germans and their myths, explains that "[d]er Volkswagen wurde zum Zeichen des Dazugehörens, und der Mercedes war das Symbol des gelungenen Aufstiegs" (the Volkswagen became a sign of belonging/inclusion, and the Mercedes was the symbol of advancement/career, the confirmation of success). "Überspitzt gesagt, löste der Mercedesstern das Eiserne Kreuz der Kriegsgeneration ab" (to exaggerate, the Mercedes star replaced the Iron Cross of the war generation), he adds (Münkler 2010, pp. 10–11).

While the relevance of certain status symbols might have changed over time, and while particular items might be of greater or lower importance in certain milieus or age groups, and *even* if "share economy" is certainly not an alien concept (when it comes to sharing music, holiday apartments, or even cars), I would still suggest that the average German has a great preference for calling things his or her own. And, if I am saying "my own," I mean I either want to *personally* possess an item or it should at least belong to "me and my spouse" or, as a rare exception, "me and my brother / sister / son / daughter." Germans greatly respect private ownership and rarely borrow or lend items. Over here, you better do not use your colleague's personal (motif) office mug without his or her express permission! If, during a meeting, you borrow a pen, even if it is an inexpensive one, make sure you don't forget to return it. It could otherwise leave a bad taste, and you could be considered careless or, in the worst case, not trustworthy.

I remember when my cousin's wife Aarti, in India, told me about how she once learned about her son's habit of eating from his kindergarten best friend's snacks. The friend's mother had already developed the habit of preparing an extra portion for little Sachin. My instant thought was that Aarti must have felt very embarrassed when she found out; however, Aarti replied: "No, not at all! This is how they learn to share!" Well, I don't think the average German parent would have seen the matter from this perspective.

Germans, when at a restaurant with friends or colleagues, have the habit of splitting the bill in a way that everyone pays for what they ordered (plus the tip). Some people would quickly get nervous if someone were to suggest sharing a bottle of water (which, in Germany, can easily cost up to seven euros), and rarely would anyone suggest just splitting the bill equally among the number of heads at the table.

The average German does not only value private ownership, but also puts great emphasis on titles; at least when he or she has one. I was once returned a letter which I, as part of a mailing campaign, had sent to a baron or monarch with a very long, complicated name and several titles of nobility. He, or maybe his personal assistant, had marked in red how I should have addressed him properly (regarding the order of the salutation). Thank God, barons and monarchs are not part of my target group anymore! However, I try to never forget to use the doctoral degree when I talk to someone with a "Dr." in their name. Maybe not every child of an academic with a doctor's degree would be reminded to add the parent's title on a postcard being sent from summer camp (I was!), but a patronizing or dismissive "für Sie immer noch Herr *Dr.* Schmidt!" (to *you*, I am still Dr. Schmidt, rather than just "Mr." Schmidt) is a phrase an inexperienced apprentice or trainee might still have to listen to at the beginning of his or her career. When watching *Tatort*, the popular German Sunday evening crime series, I am always impressed with how the police inspectors put great emphasis on introducing themselves and greeting each other with the appropriate ranks (or correct each other when they are, sometimes in a provocative fashion, up- or downgraded by salutation).

Participating in a TV discussion about the latest trials and tribulations in the grand coalition, political scientist Prof. Dr. rer. pol. habil. Dr. phil. Karl-Rudolf Korte (a simple "Professor Korte" should suffice as salutation if you meet him) recently stated that "[w]ir sind natürlich in Deutschland auch Angst-Weltmeister. ... Kein Land hat so viele Krimiserien, Angstlust am Abend treibt uns um. Und manchmal auch solche apokalyptischen Talkshows, die manchmal auch Angst unterstützen" (in Germany, of course, we are also world champions of fear. ... No country has so many crime series. Fearlust in the evening haunts us / keeps us occupied. And sometimes, also apocalyptic talk shows, that also support fear) (Westdeutscher Rundfunk Köln 2018). I am not sure if Korte is right about our supremacy in crime series, but I am almost certain he is right about the pessimistic talk shows. And, I do not doubt for one moment what he says about the almost proverbial "German Angst." "Die 'German Angst' steckt tief in unseren Genen" (the "German fear" is deep in our genes) headlines an article discussing the possible causes of the phenomenon (Czycholl 2014): "Unsere Nachbarn wissen es schon lange: Wir Deutschen sind ein Volk von Bedenkenträgern, durchleben kaum einen Tag ohne Existenzangst und hassen Veränderungen" (our neighbors have known it for a long time: We Germans are a people of doubters; we hardly live through a day without a fear of existence and we hate change), reads the text:

> *Die Deutschen sind von einem Gefühl der permanenten Bedrohung getrieben. Um dem entgegenzuwirken, haben sie schon den Sozialstaat erfunden, nehmen Dinge wie einen Reformstau billigend in Kauf und geben Milliarden für Versicherungen aus, um sich gegen praktisch jedes Risiko abzusichern, das das Leben theoretisch mit sich bringen kann.*
>
> *Ob streitwütige Nachbarn oder Einbruch, Handyverlust oder Zahnersatz, Leben und sogar Sterben – für sämtliche Eventualitäten stapeln sich die Policen in deutschen Regalen. Ausländische Kommentatoren haben für dieses Lebensgefühl längst einen Begriff gefunden: "German Angst". (Czycholl 2014)*

> *(Germans are driven by a feeling of permanent threat. To address this, they have invented the welfare state, accept things like a backlog of reforms, and spend billions on insurance to protect themselves against virtually every risk that life can theoretically present.*
>
> *Whether it's quarrelsome neighbors or burglaries, loss of mobile phones or dentures, life, and even death, policies are piled up on German shelves for all eventualities. Foreign commentators have long since found a term for this attitude to life: "German Angst.")*

"Sicherheit" (possible translations of the word are safety, security, and certainty) currently ranks fifth in the value index (Werte-Index), as researched by Peter Wippermann and Jens Krüger, and has moved up two ranks as compared to 2016. Since 2009, these regular studies, and their respective research outcomes, reflect the significance and relevance

Table 4.1 Value index 2018 (Werte-Index by Wippermann and Krüger)

Rank in 2018	Value (German)	Value (English)	Rank in 2016
1	Natur	Nature	4
2	Gesundheit	Health	1
3	Familie	Family	6
4	Freiheit	Freedom	2
5	Sicherheit	Safety / security / certainty	7
6	Erfolg	Success	3
7	Gemeinschaft	Community / companionship	5
8	Anerkennung	Recognition	8
9	Nachhaltigkeit	Sustainability	10
10	Gerechtigkeit	Justice or fairness	9

of the values of German web users (79 percent of all Germans above the age of 14 years are active users), while also highlighting developments and trends. Table 4.1 shows how often, and in which contexts, 10 basic values were discussed in German-language social media (Wippermann and Krüger 2017, p. 6).

The authors of the study explain that, alongside "Familie" and "Natur," the relevance of the value "Sicherheit" has been increasing in the researched context, and they have especially observed an increase in articles / contributions that have a political security context. The focus of these texts or contributions has been on the role of the State, especially in connection with the so-called refugee crisis. As the authors explain, the focus has been both on issues of internal security and on the security of refugees, which must be guaranteed. "Freiheit" has been declining, and the term has been discussed in the context of personal freedom (lifestyle, and so on), rather than political freedom. "Erfolg" has seen a steep decline, from rank three to rank number six. "The era of heroes seems to be over," conclude Wippermann and Krüger (2018, pp. 6–7), contemplating that Generation Z, youngsters born between 1995 and 2010, would rather count on hard work than heroism. "But this is accompanied by a great desire for predictability," they add.

What We Trust in: Plans, Rules, and Clear-cut Directions

I agree that, overall, Germans like things to be foreseeable, and they would rather avoid uncertainty. We (quickly) tend to feel uneasy when things are either unpredictable or they are not going as planned; making detailed plans makes us feel (more) comfortable, even if we picture ourselves in worst-case scenarios. Great focus is put on problem analysis, and for a German, it is often more important to know *why* things went wrong, rather than to (quickly) fix a problem. For example, when I once complained (*yes*, I did …) that a newspaper was not delivered to my room in the morning—as promised in the hotel's special offer—the receptionist consulted her computer and made several attempts to find out *how* that could have happened, before offering me an issue just from the newspaper rack in the lobby. And, I truly appreciated her efforts…

When dealing with a German for the first time, Katharina Bömers, Project Manager Training International at a local chamber of commerce's academy, suggests being flexible, "because 'the German' is often not flexible." We are not very used to coping with the unexpected; since everybody pretty much sticks to the rules, most of the time, things are "under control." The standard German household does not employ a driver who might not show up in the morning because of some personal issues (we do not have drivers at all!). Only very rarely would heavy rains or snowstorms foil our plans—and if it happens, we are in a perceived state of national emergency, and the weather conditions are all over the news. Even our mothers-in-law have limited power … hardly anybody would show up late to a meeting because she requested a favor.

Travel writer Cal O Cal, who spends quite some time each year in Munich, where I met him, summarized his best practices for dealing with Germans as follows: "Make a plan, explain the plan to them, and stick to the plan. Then, invite them for a beer. Any changes to the plan will confuse them. Germans like planning."

Munich-based Senior Project Manager Hasan Syed remarked to me that he sometimes struggles with how Germans plan for social meetings, or even business meetings, *months* in advance. "I understand why, as it is efficient," he says, "but last minute social or business gatherings are common in other countries, including the UK, where I am from."

When asking people who travel a lot or work internationally to share their respective experiences, it didn't come as a surprise to me that the Germans' direct way of communicating was mentioned several times. However, I was shocked to learn how *irritating* some styles of behavior can seem for many foreigners; "When dealing with Germans for the very first time, it was challenging to understand why they are so serious, humorless, unfriendly, and rude," Manoj Barve, a consultant from India who has been living and working in Germany for some years, said to me. What Barve still struggles with are the (what he describes as) cold, or less-emotional, relationships with neighbors and colleagues. However, he adds that "you will realize that Germans are extremely self-critical, down-to-earth, egalitarian, socially conscious, and environmentally responsible people. They are also friendly, helpful, and humorous, but it may take a couple of years to realize that." A gentleman from the United Kingdom finds it difficult that "Germans are also often eager to offer their personal view of things, even when not invited to do so, at times." Kuldeep Saraswat, a nationalized German, who works as a supply chain manager, told me how sometimes, in Germany, he struggles because of "too much directness. In these situations, I find Germans too technical-thinking, lacking the emotional part of situations," he said. According to artist Rena Dumont, Germans do not rely very much on their gut instincts, but would rather approach things intellectually.

Germans like to spell out things and prefer to put, or have things put, in writing. "No matter how small the matter is, the minutes are mostly taken!" an Indian CEO observed, about his business meetings with Germans. An alumni participant of an international exchange program for managers (whom I had interviewed for one of my e-books on trade shows) observed that, in Germany, the "responses from companies are very straightforward." The managing director from Indore said that "it's good to be straight to the point but sometimes, it takes a longer discussion to convey objective." People from so-called high-context cultures (such as Asia or South America) typically put more emphasis on relationships (more than Germans, the Swiss, or people from Scandinavian countries). They generally have great antennae for how something is said and need much more contextual information, which I would assume, can take more time to convey or gather. They generally would want to know: Who are they talking to? How is the person related to them, their company, or their colleagues? What role does he or she play in the organization?

Germans, however, have been socialized in a low-context culture; we are generally interested in facts and procedures. We rely on the professional expertise the other person has and tend to take words literally. We do not rely on contextual elements (i.e., the speaker's tone of voice or body language) to communicate information and speak clearly about what is important to us. Clear messages are generally expected and appreciated; ambiguity makes us nervous. German native Tina Oreskovich recommends "communicating clearly and directly—otherwise, we get confused." Englishman Adam Fletcher, who is living with his German girlfriend in Berlin, explains in his book *How to be German*: "English is not about what you say, but how you say it. German is both, but more the former." He elaborates: "[W]hat Germans say tends to be direct and prepared with minimal ambiguity. Ruthlessly efficient, if you will. In English, for example, if you want someone to do something for you, you do not merely go up to that person and ask them to do something for you ...[Germans] just say 'I need this, do it, by this date. Alles klar?' then walk off" (Fletcher 2015, pp. 27–28).

Germans distinguish between a professional and private sphere, and that (also) makes them less vulnerable to criticism. For instance, if someone told me that a major aspect was missing in my book, I would not feel he or she is criticizing me as a person; people are just commenting on my work and helping me to improve the outcome! And, since we are on the subject, several people in my network have been pointing out how Germans (think they) "know everything better than other people," as someone with a bi-cultural background (half-German) put it. The following subtle criticism inherent in the quote from a gentleman from the United Kingdom might not be so evident for those Germans who are (generally) not trained to read between the lines: "Ever since I first started dealing with Germans, I have found them to be a highly educated, culturally interested people who have a (sometimes unhealthy) portion of self-confidence and who are always willing to give people their opinions." Typically, Germans convey any doubts very frankly, not trying to cover anything up or thinking about how their comments might be (perceived as) tactless or insulting. *Not* to tell the other person what they think would make them feel like they are being dishonest. Wouldn't the other person deserve to hear the (i.e., their) truth? However, many Germans would still be hesitant to tell their bosses that their Christmas party was boring or inform their clients that they find their constant queries annoying! I will talk about how Germans (like to) communicate at greater length in Chapter 5.

Another British gentleman pointed out how, even after having lived in Germany for 25 years, he can never get used to the use of (the more colloquial) "Du," that you, in connection with first names, would address your friends and family with, and (the formal) "Sie" that, as a thumb rule, is appropriate for addressing (other) grown-ups that you are not especially close with—like your boss (Frau Drescher), new colleague (Herr Raudschus), your child's teacher, the vegetable vendor, or a ticket collector on a train. "I still confuse 'Sie' with coldness and distance," he wrote, "although I know it is a matter of respect." On the other hand, he finds it irritating that people assume "that you are a 'friend for life' just because you have invited them into your home (or vice versa)."

Stephan Janouch, a senior business development manager, who has worked extensively with people from the United States, has observed similar misunderstandings: "Germans often claim that Americans are superficial; that is, acting super-friendly without actually meaning it. Germans, on the other hand, are quite often accused of being unfriendly and brusque," he says. "This perceived social incompatibility can have a severe negative impact when trying to build a business relationship," he adds. In Janouch's experience, it generally takes a similar amount of time for Germans or Americans to befriend someone within their own community. However, getting to the state of viewing someone as a friend, in his understanding, follows different paths. In the early phase, Americans may already be acting very open and friendly (which may make Germans mistakenly believe they are already seen as friends), while Germans will remain in a more neutral behavioral state (which, for foreigners, may be incorrectly interpreted as rudeness). At a later stage, when an American might only make minor changes to his or her behavior, the German may (emotionally) open up as well, eventually being ready for real friendship.

In many cultures, people would especially (or only) trust their friends and family and *may* consider people in their extended network—that is, friends of friends of friends—especially trustworthy. That is not (so much) the case in Germany, where people tend to put (more) emphasis on other aspects: For Germans, credibility and reliability are the fundamentals of trust. We believe in institutions; people generally obey rules and adhere to norms and standards. "Qualifications on paper are often worth more than the actual skills that a person has," a gentleman from the United Kingdom working in Germany told me.

For Hasan Syed, "sticking to the rules, by the book, in all situations, especially in business," is another concept that is hard to understand. He has observed that "Germans tend to follow rules, in any context, with great discipline." Germany is a country with a strong rule of law, a low level of corruption, and low political and economic risk. People living in such environments are generally more trusting of others than those in countries with the opposite conditions (Buchan 2009, pp. 392–97); we (think we) act rationally, and in making trust judgments, affective (one could also say emotional or intuitive) influences do not (to a great extent / as compared to other cultures) take priority over cognitive influences such as professional credentials (competence). We tend to make trust decisions based on a rational weighing of cost and benefits.

What We (Try to) Teach Our Kids: Manners and Common Habits

A popular saying goes: "was Hänschen nicht lernt, lernt Hans nimmermehr;" this translates literally to "What (little) Hänschen doesn't learn, (grown-up) Hans never learns either," meaning that whatever (habits) you don't learn as a kid, you will never be able to understand/adopt. The connotation is rather patronizing, does not target grown-ups like the "you cannot teach an old dog new tricks" saying does, and is not *as* harsh as "A tree must be bent while it is young." The Hänschen quote is often used in the context of "proper behavior."

If Hänschen doesn't learn to say "please" and "thank you" (on *every* possible occasion), he will never learn. "What is the word?!" (Wie heißt das Wort?!), parents would remind Hänschen or Gretchen, when he or she requests something. "Bitte" (please) is the proper answer. "How do you say?!" (Wie sagt man?!), the parent would add, if Gretchen forgot to say, "Thank you!" In Germany, a smile or an approving gesture is generally not considered an adequate reply to express gratitude or thankfulness; if you do not utter a "Dankeschön," you might be considered unappreciative or ill-mannered.

If you wish to enter a room or borrow a pen, better (knock on the door and) ask permission. Even if you, as a guest in a small group and as the first person at the table to do so, wish to open one of the little bottles at a conference table, it is maybe not really expected, but still considered polite to first ask, "May I?"

Look the person you are talking to in the eye, no matter if it is a man or a woman, and no matter if he or she is the most senior person in the room or someone serving at your table. Maybe it is not a good idea to keep constant eye-contact with the service staff (that could be misunderstood as distraction or flirting), but when you are served the first cup of coffee, an appreciative "Thank you" and short eye-contact wouldn't harm the impression that you are considerate and appreciative. Looking the other person in the eye is a demonstration of honesty; it shows that you are paying attention, that you are self-confident, and that you are a sincere individual showing respect for the other person. What you consider "long" or "short" eye-contact depends on how you have been socialized, and the difference can be a split second. Observing how your German business partners handle such situations might help, especially with the following service-staff situation: even when Germans are somewhat hierarchical (more than their Nordic neighbors but less like, for example, people socialized in China or India), it is considered bad manners to (openly) order people around. Better to speak (what might feel for you) *especially* politely if you are used to using a different (maybe more dismissive) tone when speaking to service staff in your home country. Remember that you won't get a second chance to make a first impression, and you don't want to be misjudged because of your manners (that might be or *are* appropriate at home).

And, that includes table manners. Very likely, as kids, your German business partners were (constantly) reminded to avoid making sounds when drinking or eating; today, they would rather die from stomach pain than burp in public, and would easily get annoyed when someone slurps his or her drink, or sniffles. *We* consider it normal to blow your nose, even at a conference table or in the restaurant (I know, you might find that *disgusting*).

And, while most people know that (and admire how) people from other cultures, at home, might skillfully be using hands or chop sticks to consume their food and would, therefore, not frown upon a certain potential clumsiness when *they* use a fork and knife, the "American way" of cutting the entire meal into bite-sized pieces, to be eaten with a fork only, could cause some irritation. Over here, we use both fork and knife, cut the bites one by one, eat slowly, and do not talk with a full mouth ("Nicht mit vollem Mund sprechen!").

People usually do not share food; Herr Schneider will order his plate of schnitzel and expect you to choose a dish of your own. If Frau Friedsam offers you one of her French fries, that would imply a very relaxed (by German standards), almost intimate, relationship between the two of you (don't worry—just grab the potato stick!). You do not have to leave any food on the plate to let the host know that you are satisfied; we tell our kids that, if they do not finish their food, the next day's weather will be bad. Or parents would remind their children that "in *Africa*, children are starving!"—which might, to some extent, explain our one-sided view of the continent. When you have finished eating, leave the cutlery on the plate (knife parallel to the fork).

If you do not want to try something offered to you, you don't need to worry that you might hurt your hosts' feelings. You can either tell them that you just do not like Käsespätzle (cheese noodles) or Saumagen (stuffed pig's stomach) very much, or on the very rare occasion when you are invited to a house (refer to Chapter 7) and you cannot invoke religious reasons or some food intolerance, tell the host that your stomach is slightly upset from the journey. Only start eating when all the guests are seated. And, be prepared to make conversation. Try not to litter the table. If you accidently spill sauce on the tablecloth though, you do not have to feel embarrassed; still, as always with Germans, an "oh, I am so sorry!" will do no harm.

Although things are changing, as our society does, as a thumb rule, you should begin with the premise that Germans appreciate a calm and quiet environment; in the standard German house rules (Hausordnung), you will always find at least one paragraph stating the hours of the day (and night) in which you are not supposed to let your children or your stereo system play loudly, use a drilling machine, vacuum clean the floor, take a shower, or use the washing machine. I have heard of residential communities where you are not allowed to use the toilet flush at night! So, when you are, for example, waiting in the entrance hall of a company, better keep it down.

When talking to others, take care to let them finish their sentences. Germans are very used to sequential speaking (other than like, for example, people who converse in Spanish and do not seem to mind everyone speaking at the same time). Interrupting or talking over someone when the other person hasn't finished his or her sentence can, on many occasions, be considered rude. However, taking notes is always a good idea and indicates that you are listening closely and that you are interested. Depending on your counterparts' age group, preferably use paper and pen; if you use your (muted!) phone for taking notes, people might think you are distracted.

Germans show their emotions less than people from many other countries, whether it is joy, excitement, or sadness; however, we are quite free with expressing our frustration. "Ein Indianer kennt keinen Schmerz" (an American Indian doesn't know pain) is some nonsense many (still) like to tell boys when they cry. A woman who cries after a quarrel with a colleague is considered unprofessional and weak. Men are not supposed to cry at all!

During office hours, we "talk business" and are (more or less) focused on getting things done. That doesn't mean that we don't exchange some pleasantries or wouldn't congratulate our colleague for his or her birthday or work anniversary (sometimes the department would even make the effort to buy a joint present!); however, it is a common understanding that work should always come first. "Erst die Arbeit, dann das Vergnügen" (business before pleasure) is the directive.

Now and then, colleagues may go out for a drink after work, while still generally taking care not to tell their workmates too much about their personal lives. It is possible to befriend a colleague, and as far as I know, there is no such thing as labeling or banning affairs at the workplace as "illicit" (unless you work for the Catholic Church). However, it is (still) considered more advisable to separate the private life from the business sphere: "Dienst ist Dienst, und Schnaps ist Schnaps!" (business is business, and booze is booze).

When you leave the office, you wish your colleagues a nice "Feierabend;" the term cannot really be translated, and over time, has come to mean that the evening is for leisure and recreation, and that *now* is the time to rest and be yourself. Only *then* would a (mainstream) German show certain (maybe more cheerful or down-to-earth) aspects of his or her personality.

Some other core principles that we were all (generally) taught are to be on time and to stick to what you promise or commit to. The sticking to (former) decisions or statements might sometimes come across as inflexibility. While somewhere else people may make decisions, bearing in mind that those decisions may need to be altered or adapted along the way, Germans typically view a decision akin to a promise that has to be kept, no matter what happens. "A clear communication on which decisions are meant to be solid versus 'intermediate' decisions which are made based on limited data sets and will probably need refining is key to avoiding a poisoning of the hopefully fruitful business relationship," Senior Business Development Manager Stephan Janouch advises.

While, for my friends from France, philosophy was a mandatory course at school, where they could debate the countless facets of life and its truths (at least, that is what I imagine), I had to endlessly write expositions/considerations (Erörterungen), listing the pros and cons of certain matters (e.g., "Should cigarette advertising be completely banned?") to arrive at (final, cast in stone) conclusions. The better you could argue in favor of *one* right (or wrong), the greater was the applause. And, we were taught that it is better not to use a conjunctive in letters and reports. For example, instead of "I would be delighted to welcome you to my birthday party," one should rather write, "I look forward to welcoming you to my birthday party," because that sounds much more convinced and convincing!

And, we are told to do *one* thing at a time ("Eine Sache nach der anderen!") and "alles zu seiner Zeit" (all in good time). And, for us, it is "normal" to be *on* time. People who tend to be late are "abnormal," and based on a very common understanding, need to be admonished or avoided. Having understood that, it might not come as a surprise to you that Germany ranks as one of the top countries worldwide when it comes to the stress we put on punctuality ("Pünktlichkeit"). In business, arriving even a few minutes late (without a *very* good excuse) will create a bad impression. If you think a "Sorry, I was held up at another meeting!" is a very good excuse, forget it! Also, telling me that when coming from the airport during rush hour, it had unfortunately taken you more than the anticipated 10 minutes to arrive in the city center won't make things better.

Normally, in business, I would expect you to arrive at my office some five to 10 minutes before the fixed timing (and ask my assistant to let you wait until the clock strikes whatever hour we have agreed upon). On the other hand, at a trade show, while people would expect you to show up at 10:00 a.m. sharp, for example, a delay of five minutes would usually not be frowned upon. However, if you are running more than five minutes late, better give your appointment a call and inform him or her of where you are and confirm that you are on your way. Maybe they will offer to reschedule or try to meet you halfway.

"After coming back from a long business trip to India, where things might not go as you want or not always as planned," a German gentleman recently told me, "I was waiting for a train in Germany. It was fascinating to see how a delay of two or three minutes made everyone completely nervous, or even anxious, that they might run late for something." He continued saying "the reactions were also very interesting, as many became angry within these few minutes and started complaining. First world problems, I'd say."

CHAPTER 5

How to Talk to Germans

How Culture Matters: Let's (not just) Cut the Small Talk

For your first meeting with Germans, intercultural coach Andrew MacKichan would advise: "Be on time, be smart, be prepared, and be clear about your goals. Shake hands firmly, look them in the eyes, and cut the small talk." In my opinion, if you follow MacKichan's advice, you have indeed heeded the most important aspects to make a good start. Senior Project Manager Hasan Syed would add that it "is important not to make humorous comments and opinionated statements. Unlike in London, this is not appreciated." "Germans enjoy humor," he continues, but in his experience, "it takes time to develop the trust to start using it. Do not be over confident, regardless of context, and most importantly, be humble and genuine." While it is recommendable to (quickly) get to the point, it doesn't mean that you skip the small talk entirely. When you meet someone at a fair, a good opening question is "How has the fair been so far?" When you welcome someone at your office, a simple "I hope you had a good trip?" might trigger a brief informal opening conversation, during which you can get a glimpse of your counterpart's personality and give him or her the chance to warm up to you. Still, if people ask you how *your* trip was, try to keep it short. Maybe, if the meeting goes well, more pleasantries can be exchanged when the task at hand (to discuss what is on the agenda) has been completed.

Nevertheless, when people from diverse backgrounds meet, things often seem to work out somehow anyway, don't they? For instance, it is fascinating how people from different countries, but with the same professional background, can communicate "sufficiently," even if they hardly speak any English (or maybe Spanish as another lingua franca). Ever since I worked for a Chinese electronics company and observed

German engineers, equipped with very rudimentary English skills, discussing printed circuit boards with my client (who was not exactly fluent either), I have called that "getting along with PCB-English." The focus on "business" and the ability to exchange thoughts easily lead to the conclusion that culture hardly matters; far from it!

Very often, in doing business (or trying to do business), the impact of culture is tremendously underestimated. To successfully deal with Germans (or people from other cultures in general), one needs to internalize a lot more than just a few common habits or dos and don'ts. It is advisable to consciously reflect on one's own habits, values, and beliefs, and try to set what one feels in contrast to what has been learned about "the Other." How else could you be aware that what you perceive as "normal" or "standard procedure" can cause great irritation, and finally, spoil the deal? A German-speaking Scandinavian businessperson addressing his or her visitor from Germany with (the rather informal) "Du" might wonder why the latter suddenly seems a bit tense. Someone who sends an e-mail addressing his or her prospective German sales lead with "Hi" should not necessarily expect a response. On the other hand, a German might wonder why his or her Japanese client doesn't reply to the brief request addressed to "Dear Yuki!" If you have skipped Chapter 4, I suggest you catch up on what you have missed.

Some things that may be considered polite where you come from may not be considered so in Germany. For example, in some cultures, people may refuse to accept what is offered to them, like tea/coffee, drinks, gifts, help, and so on, but if insisted upon, they may accept them. In Germany, people are used to take things very straightforwardly, so if you initially say "no" to something being offered (e.g., a cup of tea), it would very likely be understood as a "no." This could require some readjustment in the thought process. However, if you are lucky, your German host might have made some effort to learn about your (culture's) way of doing things and would still insist on you have something to drink. Which reminds me of how I felt slightly puzzled when, during a visit to Dubai, my Emirati client, after my initial "no," did *not* insist on serving me tea, which I would have *really* loved to try.

Looking at "over-adjustment," MacKichan observed something similar during a workshop, with British and German participants, that focused on their intercultural team working; "the Germans were acting like stereotypical Brits (going off-piste, telling jokes, lack of focus) and the Brits like stereotypical Germans (goal focused, time obsessed)." MacKichan told me how this continued until one of the British participants noticed what was going on, and this became a great learning point.

But yes, Germans usually want a conversation to be very focused; their expectation would be that the person they are talking to should concentrate on them only. So, when you have important matters to discuss, always try to have a one-on-one conversation. The "more the merrier" approach that you might want to follow during trade shows or conferences, by inviting more parties to mix and mingle, might make Germans shy away. A German's perception could be that he or she is not important to you (why else would you be talking to others?); a German might even consider the behavior disrespectful (although the tolerance level for distractions is usually higher at trade fairs).

However, when you picture "the" (archetype) German, please do not imagine only a white male person. In Germany, there are people with all kinds of backgrounds. Somebody who hands you a business card with the name Abdullah on it might be the grandson of a Turkish immigrant, born and bred in a small town in hinterland Bavaria, and be "more papist than the Pope" when it comes to straightforwardness and task orientation.

Although women are still not equally represented in top leading positions, chances are high that the woman you are talking to has the power to give or deny a "Go ahead!" If, as a man, you are used to mainly doing business with men, take care not to offend (German) women by leaving them out of the conversation and / or spoiling the deal by ignoring them entirely. Even if it makes you feel uneasy, try to look them in the eye and offer/ accept a firm handshake. The golden rule "Ladies first" does not apply in a business context; I would advise that you (try to) start with greeting the highest-ranking person—for example, the managing director—and then proceed to those below him or her in rank. If there are just too many people in the room to straightforwardly proceed to the most important person (according to hierarchy), or in case you find it difficult to figure out the rank order, start with the person standing closest to you and do greet all one by one (e.g., going sequentially from left to right). You can still pay the most senior person more attention when shaking his or her hand.

Giving some thought to the extent to which (different) hierarchical structures might play a role for you and your counterpart, in a project team, for instance, is advisable: No matter how hierarchical your business partner's company is structured (within Germany that will also vary, depending on the company size and maturity in the market, for example), your German counterpart may easily get annoyed if even little demands in day-to-day business were channeled through his or her superior.

The way people from all over the world think about (if at all) or conceive of time can vary greatly, and this is another major source of misunderstandings and frustration (Schugk 2004, p. 149). A Pakistani buyer who expects his or her German supplier to drop everything when paying a surprise visit might easily feel dumbstruck when told that "unfortunately, now is not a good time." For some, approaching project steps in a sequential fashion, completing one task after another, doing one thing at a time, and sticking to the schedule are very important matters; such understanding is typically called a linear time concept. Germans overall (unconsciously) very much subscribe to that concept, and to a greater or lesser extent, so do people from Switzerland, Japan, or the United States, for example. For many others, like people living in Russia, Mexico, China, Saudi Arabia, and India, the focus is more on adaptability and flexibility, and they approach project steps in a (more) fluid manner; many things are dealt with at once, and interruptions are accepted (Meyer 2015, p. 39).

How we perceive time can play an important role in business, and one should reflect upon what is (generally) more important for themselves and their business partners: to concentrate on the task at hand (a behavior correlating with a linear time concept), or to establish and maintain a good relationship (subscribing to the overall idea that time is flexible). For a German, "maintaining a good relationship" could, however, very often spell out as: always deliver on time and don't forget to send along a bottle of wine with the annual Christmas card (more on the topic will be explained in Chapter 7).

For establishing and preserving a good relationship, you must keep your promises and let people know when there is a problem. If you have grown up in an environment where people are reluctant to give somebody bad news, listen carefully: Over here, if something goes wrong, went wrong, or is about to go wrong, you need to push the panic button

(Achtung!) and tell your German contact. You realize that you won't be able to ship the samples as promised? Tell your contact, so they can adapt their planning accordingly. You won't be able to place your order right now, since your boss objects? Tell me, so I don't hold back the stock for you any longer. Also, if you messed up (no matter whether you are personally responsible, or your supplier has goofed up), give Germans the certainty that you understand that they are in trouble now; very often, an apology will be expected. If you do not feel comfortable saying "sorry, that was clearly my fault"—whether for cultural or legal reasons—at least acknowledge the difficulty your contact must be in, and tell them in detail what you will do to ensure the problem gets solved. If they do not want to listen to the details, don't press too hard. But, a "simple" (as we would perceive it) "we still can fix it!" most certainly won't do the job.

For Germans, processes need to be crystal-clear; even if you are still at a very early stage in discussing business opportunities, be ready to answer questions concerning the remote future. As Sylvia Schroll-Machl points out in her book, *Doing Business with Germans: Their Perception, Our Perception*, Germans, being perfectionists, appreciate great attention to detail:

> [I]t is characteristic that Germans make exact and detailed plans, minimize possible sources of errors beforehand, are well prepared for meetings and negotiations […]. In order to reach [their] goals of perfection, it is important not to make approximations but to follow the guidelines and norms exactly. (Schroll-Machl 2008, pp. 78–79)

One could also say that Germans lack flexibility. "Don't worry! We'll see!" is definitely not what your buyer is eager to hear. Schroll-Machl suggests that you should be aware that Germans are not "directing their obsession with rules and norms against you personally, or trying to be patronising. They are just being 'professional,' as they see it." One could be comforted by the fact that Germans act the same way toward each other as well (ibid. p. 85).

What irritates me is when a new business contact (simply) tells me that he or she has an extensive network, and that he or she would be happy to suggest a mutually beneficial business relationship. I want to know: "What is your occupation? What exactly are you doing? What is it you expect from me? How can we work together—do you have a (business) plan?" By the way, be careful about suggesting a "joint venture" to the German you just met. We are likely to understand it as a "Joint Venture (JV)"—a construct with full-fledged legal and financial implications. It is better to suggest cooperation instead.

Be Aware: Things (that) Could Get Lost in Translation

Even if the Germans you are talking to speak English at some advanced level, be aware that there is still plenty of room for linguistic misunderstandings; here are some (initial) examples of what can go wrong (I will be digging deeper into the subject in Chapter 6).

First of all, you should keep in mind that if people are not fluent in English (or any language), very often, they would translate anything said in a foreign tongue word by word. Because Germans also tend to take everything said literally, a friendly "Hi! How are you doing?" can really disconcert some. The "Hi" can easily be perceived as too informal (am I your buddy?!), and some Germans might feel that they should seriously answer a question about their well-being. We ask the same question ("Wie geht's?"), but only when we already know somebody and then we have all the possible answers at hand (Germans would very often say "Geht so. Viel Arbeit"—"I am okay. Lots of work to do"). I would suggest that you instead say "good morning," "good afternoon," or simply "hello."

A German living and working in the United Kingdom observed how, sometimes, Germans just translate their slogans (word for word) and expect the British to understand them. He said to me, "This does not always work; for example, when labeling rucksacks (Rucksäcke) as 'body bags' (Leichensäcke)." One of my German course participants told me how, during an international conference, he felt slightly embarrassed when he realized that he was not supposed to have "a date" with his potential client, but "an appointment." He had just translated "Verabredung," a term you can use for a romantic meeting or business luncheon. A retired claims manager mentioned a potential pitfall that can happen in his former field of work, especially when English is not the mother tongue of both parties: "In the insurance industry," he explained to me, "'recoveries' can mean loss mitigation by claims management actions as well as pure collection of funds." I have no idea what the first one means, but it sounds like it could cost you dearly if you mixed up the terms!

Realizing that you are talking at cross-purposes with one another (although you're both using the same words) is still one of the greatest challenges in (intercultural) communication for me. A Finnish client once wanted me to assess whether his company's service would also sell in Germany. When he and his colleagues explained their business model in detail, I told them that, based on my gut feeling and (at the time still) very cursory knowledge of the market in question, I believed that a certain aspect of their business model could be a deal-breaker because, I said, "Germans think more long term." All three gentlemen looked puzzled and explained that my point was not valid because "Finns also think very long term." It was only some weeks later, when I presented the results of my research, that it turned out that when I was thinking "12–24 months," my client's association with "long-term" was three months!

Let me give you another example: I was explaining to one of my prospects how Germans tend to be very risk-averse, and how we "have lots of insurance policies." "So do we; Allianz is *very* big in India," my contact from Pune replied. What followed was a back and forth involving him trying to convince me that Indians tend to put *as* much emphasis on insurance as Germans do (my world was shaken!), and my firm conviction to the contrary. Only when I gave an example, telling my prospective client that, among many other policies, most probably 99 percent of Germans have Haftpflichtversicherung (liability insurance), and that if I accidentally smashed his TV set, the insurance would pay for it, he gave in, admitting that he had never heard of such a (weird) thing. When talking about insurance, he had thought of "life insurance."

Fons Trompenaars, a Dutch organizational theorist, management consultant, and author in the field of cross-cultural communication, and his colleague Charles Hampden-Turner highlight that

> *[i]n every culture in the world such phenomena as authority, bureaucracy, creativity, good fellowship, verification, and accountability are experienced in different ways. That we use the same words to describe*

> *them tends to make us unaware that our cultural biases and our accustomed conduct may not be appropriate, or shared. (Trompenaars and Hampden-Turner 2012, p. 4)*

Giving examples and asking questions can be a good strategy to narrow-down potential misunderstandings. "When you talk about bureaucratic hurdles, what exactly can we expect and how do you suggest we handle the matter?" I would, for instance, ask, trying to find out whether we (just) need to set aside plenty of time (whatever *plenty of time* means…), are required to talk to a grumpy official in a worn out fleece pullover who has hopefully already had his or her coffee, must not forget to pull a token number from the machine in the waiting room … or something else entirely.

I think it has already been established that, when you ask a German for his or her opinion, you should be prepared for their brutally honest opinion and a lengthy discussion about it, and that we like to state our opinions, even if not asked for it. Germans are used to voicing their viewpoints freely, without caring about someone losing his or her face. A German, for example, might frankly tell you how he or she finds it hilarious, if not moronic, how "you guys from the U.S." constantly talk in (what we perceive as) superlatives. If, in Germany, someone is happy with our work, it would never occur to him or her to tell us that we did an "awesome" job. "Awesome" for us sounds like "super-duper, ultra-mega good." In fact, as long as you don't hear a complaint, you can generally assume your boss or client is happy with the work result. "Not scolded is praise enough" (nicht geschimpft ist gelobt genug) is the overall philosophy. Of course, what some might not consider is that, "in the United States, everyone is a winner and is praised all the time," as a German native in charge of winning clients from the North American market told me. "Not so much in Germany," she said. Feedback in Germany is traditionally very direct. While somewhere else, negative feedback might be embedded (or hidden) in a positive frame ("A was pretty good, but B …"), Germans tend to focus on the core message ("B was not good enough").

Manoj Barve, who knows very well how Germans (overall) tick, suggests that, when you praise a German, "compliment him or her but also balance it by saying 'but.' Everybody likes compliments but, if you don't have *some* reservations, it will make them suspicious!" That is *so* true! I remember how, some years ago, about two weeks into my new job, my boss casually said to me in the coffee kitchen, "I really liked how you introduced yourself and your area of responsibility in the meeting this morning." My immediate thought was, "Oh my God, what did I do wrong?" But Michaela just smiled, and after pouring her coffee, left. And that was it! She was really an exceptional manager.

The most amusing episode UK management Consultant Sue De'Ath remembers while working with Germans was when, as an introduction to a workshop, she asked the participants to think of two truths and one lie. "The literal nature of the language and mind meant the response was either obvious or they could not state a lie," she said.

Yes, you can have great fun when working with Germans. However, I would still recommend avoiding making humorous statements. I do not subscribe to the idea that Germans are entirely devoid of humor, but what we perceive as funny is sometimes just very different from what *you* would find refreshing: "Two types of jokes are to my eyes very German," I was once told by a French lady who is married to a German; "Practical jokes, at the cost of someone, and the use of sarcasm and calling it irony," she explained. "If I react negatively to the joke, the most common reaction is being told that *I* have no humor."

So, don't mention the war and don't try to be funny! You don't find my remark funny? Q.E.D (quod erat demonstrandum, which was to be proven).

CHAPTER 6

What to Expect in Typical Business Encounters

What You Should Know About German Trade Shows

German trade shows are the place to be if you want to learn about the latest technologies, update yourself on international market trends, and meet potential business partners from all over the world. According to the Association of the German Trade Fair Industry (AUMA), around two-thirds of the world's leading trade fairs take place in Germany. Every year, around 150 international trade fairs and exhibitions are hosted in the very heart of Europe, attended by 180,000 exhibitors and around 10 million visitors (Riemhofer 2017). Very often, visiting one of the shows is the very first step companies would take to explore the German/European market, and it is quite likely that even *your* first visit to Germany is taking place in this context.

Very often, trade fair participants are in awe when they visit a show in Germany for the first time; they are not only impressed by the size, but also the professionalism. Here are a few examples of some of the top events:

The world's most important motor show, the *IAA,* has a long history; the first show took place in 1897 at a hotel in Berlin. Since 1951, the bi-annual event has been hosted in Frankfurt. Although the 2017 event saw a decline in both visitors and exhibitors, the organizer, *Verband der Automobilindustrie e.V.* (VDA), could still count "around 1,000" exhibitors from 39 countries (1,103 in 2015) and approximately 810,000 visitors (a fall of 13 percent as compared with the last event). The show offered nearly 200,000 square meters of exhibition space (approximately 2.2 million square feet). *IAA 2017* hosted 363 innovations, including 228 world premieres—according to the organizer, both figures are new records (Verband der Automobilindustrie e.V. (VDA) 2017).

bauma is the leading platform for experts who deal with construction and building-material machines, construction vehicles, construction equipment, and mining machines; the Munich show is held every three years. In 2016, the show covered more than 605 square meters (6.5 million square feet), and 3,425 exhibitors and 583,736 visitors attended the event (Messe München GmbH n.d.). I was very impressed when I visited *bauma CONEXPO INDIA 2015*, but was overwhelmed when I entered the Munich fairground in 2016 to meet the company I assisted in selling their concrete flooring machines during the German show.

AGRITECHNICA is the leading trade fair for agricultural machinery. The bi-annual show, which covers 23 halls, lasts for seven days; the event in 2017 set the stage for 2,802 exhibitors from 52 countries. More than 457,000 visitors attended the event, with 24 percent being international guests from altogether 128 countries (DLG Service GmbH n.d.).

Even more international and famous is *HANNOVER MESSE*. As a tradition, the Chancellor inaugurates this annual show for industrial technology; Germans can follow the opening event on the news. Every year, a partner country is featured in the show.

An event that is also extensively covered by (almost) all German media channels is the annual book fair, *Frankfurter Buchmesse* (*FBM*). In 2018, more than 7,500 exhibitors were present at the show (Frankfurter Buchmesse GmbH 2018). *FBM* is not only an exhibition—it is, by far, the best networking opportunity in the industry.

If you are into computer and video games, don't miss *gamescom* in Cologne; launched only 10 years ago, the 2018 show attracted 370,000 visitors from 114 countries, including 31,200 trade visitors (Taylor 2018).

As with everything in life, nothing is carved in stone. For example, one of the biggest shows, *CeBIT* (now *CEBIT*), has recently been undergoing a re-launch due to its shifting (or adjusting) focus. This global event for digital business, from 2018 onward, takes place in June, rather than March. To make sure you do not miss such important information, you should sign-up for newsletters that will keep you updated and follow the events on social media channels.

If you want to know which event best suits *your* needs, the free-of-charge AUMA trade fair online database is a good starting point for your research: https://auma.de/en/exhibit/find-your-exhibitions (click on "Advanced search"). I recommend that you run your search by industry or using (predefined) industry search terms. The events in the search results marked with an "int" are international events, meaning that a minimum of 10 percent are foreign exhibitors and at least five percent of the trade visitors are from abroad.

For example, if you are from the electronics industry, you might want to consider participating in *electronica* in Munich. The database presents all the relevant information such as when the next event will be taking place, who is organizing it, and what the main product groups are. You will also find certified key figures on the exhibition hall size (in square meters) and the number of visitors and exhibitors (domestic and foreign) at past events. If you want to know where the visitors have been coming from, this is where you will find the numbers. As an exhibitor, please keep in mind that trade fairs generally do not count "unique visitors," but the number of entries; meaning that people who visited the fair on both days would have been counted twice. If—as a visitor—you are especially looking for products "Made in Germany," you might be interested to know that, in 2016, 964 local exhibitors had registered for *electronica*. However, these figures include German distributors of international brands and international companies that had registered their booth via their German branch office.

This data is certified by FKM—the Society of Voluntary Control of Fair and Exhibition Statistics. In the FKM Trade Visitors Profile section (which is further down on the same page), you can also find information on the economic sectors that the visitors represent, the size of their companies/organizations, and their areas of responsibility—to give you just a few examples. The data can (also) be relevant for visitors because these figures are a good indicator of the extent to which they "fit into the picture." Very few German organizers do not support the work of AUMA to the "usual extent" (as they put it) (AUMA 2015); hence, when looking up their events, you will find very limited information (e.g., *Frankfurter Buchmesse*, *IAA*, and *ACHEMA*).

Let me also give you some very hands-on advice: as a visitor, don't forget to make sure you get access to the show. Many shows limit entrance to trade visitors only. In most cases, you don't have to prove that you are a relevant visitor, but if, for example, you want to attend the world's largest trade show for the sports business, *ISPO MUNICH*, you need a written proof of a business relationship with one of the exhibitors or an invitation issued by one of them to enter the halls. Similarly, *Spielwarenmesse* strictly limits fairground access to people who can prove they are professionally dealing with toys. It is always advisable to check the event websites and affiliated offers in advance.

Organizers constantly improve the tools they make available to the visitors; in most cases, you will find an extensive online exhibitor list, along with detailed search criteria that reflect the industry, as well as the search parameters that a visitor might use. In the weeks leading up to an event, the exhibitor databases are normally updated daily with the present state of bookings. When deciding whether or not you should visit a show, find out what the official deadline is for exhibitors to register; it may still be too early to get a good idea of who is going to be there.

Very often, trade show apps for mobile devices are offered; see whether you can synchronize the favorites that you have highlighted in the exhibitor list with the mobile application. Some shows offer a matchmaking tool that helps you network with relevant trade show participants. And, no matter how well prepared I am, when I arrive at a show, I always grab a hall plan or one of the handy trade show guides, offered for free at the entrance, for quick reference. If you cannot find the print media available, ask for it at one of the information counters that you will usually find in the halls.

For one Indian gentleman living in Canada, the greatest challenges when visiting fairs in Germany are finding a hotel close to the venue and getting tasty food at the show. If you need plenty of sleep and don't like using crowded trains and buses, make your arrangements early and be ready to pay a fat premium for your accommodation. If you cannot operate without a proper, tasty, yummy, spicy lunch, the bad news is … you won't survive. Better stay home or—as a last resort—bring your stock of chutney or chili sauce to drown whatever you get at the fair. If you are vegan, very often you will have the choice between trying to explain the concept to the staff at the snack counters (with a crowd of hungry, impatient people at your back) and hoping that they have at least a tomato and lettuce leaf left for you … or nothing. According to my superficial knowledge in that area, buns and pretzels very often contain eggs or other animal products, so don't fall for that well-meant offer; better look out for some fruit and nuts. If you need to find a prayer room, or fancy buying a five-foot tall Philodendron, or even a 65-inch Ultra HD Smart OLED TV at the show, that's probably much easier than not having to compromise on food!

Keep in mind that, if a fair lasts for three days, the second day is typically the most frequented; if the show is from Tuesday to Friday, expect Wednesday and Thursday to be very busy. Some would recommend that you should show up early on the first day because stand staff is "hungrier" then. On Friday, exhibitors might be more casual and relaxed, and you shouldn't be surprised if some start packing up and leaving Friday early afternoon—a very bad habit indeed! If you visit *Frankfurter Buchmesse*, try to wrap up your work by Friday afternoon—on Saturday and Sunday, the show is flooded with private visitors.

Don't leave applying for your visa to the last minute; remember that the trade fair organizer will also need time to issue your invitation letter or any other needed document; make sure you keep yourself informed regarding these requirements.

When packing your briefcase, remember to carry only the bare necessities; typically, it should hold your entry ticket, business cards, notepad and pen, a small bottle that you can refill with water from the tap if you like (tap water is superb in most German cities), maybe headache pills, blister plaster, and last but not least, your paper or digital battle plan. Also, don't forget that, depending on where you got your device from, you will need a plug adapter to charge your phone or laptop. Even if restaurants and the on-site supermarkets accept credit cards, having at least 20 euros in your pocket for minor expenses will help. If you want to leave the premises to have a quick bite outside the fairground, make sure you'll be granted re-entry before leaving.

Remember that Germans love rules, and if you (also) consider their guidelines important and follow them (please!), they'll love you even more. Plus, I wouldn't want you to get in trouble! Finding the best way to bend the rules and create a bypass is not a virtue admired in Germany. Don't try to skip the line at the box office, don't try to smuggle your friend onto the premises, don't try to talk staff into letting you access the fair before it officially starts, don't smoke in the washrooms (go outside and dispose of your cigarette butts in the ashtrays placed outside the halls), don't bring your own food to the restaurant, and so on.

And, please also keep in mind this rule: generally, you are not allowed to take pictures or shoot videos of exhibits and stands on the exhibition grounds unless you have first asked the exhibitor for permission to do so, and the exhibitor has explicitly granted such permission; you may even need approval from the organizer. An unsolicited "snapshot" taken at an industrial goods show can easily lead to a heavy fine. Exhibitors do not appreciate having their new developments being exposed to the spotlight.

How to Arrange for (Sales) Meetings

Some time ago, when I had a discussion with one of my clients regarding how we could keep track of the appointments to take place at his booth during a very busy annual fair in Germany (we were both scheduling meetings, and my concern was to avoid double-bookings), my client suggested that there was no need to synchronize our agendas because, according to him, we could always let one person wait for 10 minutes or so (limiting the conversation with the other prospect to 10 minutes?!). Not the greatest of ideas, if you ask me ... especially when dealing with Germans. My *standard* German reaction as a visitor put on hold would be: "Are you kidding me?," "Am I not welcome?," or "How can I rely on you if you cannot even get your schedule straight?"

In his book, *Erfolgreich akquirieren auf Messen*, which deals with how to successfully win clients during trade shows, German Sales Trainer Dirk Kreuter uses a very pointed picture to indicate what a person (over here typically) would be feeling when you make him or her wait. The man in the line drawing is checking his wristwatch; from his facial expression and body language displayed, you can sense that he is under a lot of pressure. A TNT bomb with a lit fuse in the thought bubble completes the picture (Kreuter 2014, p. 145). No matter if it is during a trade show or on the occasion of your visiting clients and prospects during a business trip through Germany, please keep in mind that Germans put great emphasis on scheduling their work, and being late or letting somebody else wait would leave a very bad first impression.

Hasan Syed advises that you should always arrive on time for a meeting or gathering. “Do not plan things less than one week in advance,” he says. “Ideally, give it at least two weeks, or longer. Over here, I have meetings scheduled for five months in the future in my calendar, which I never had in London.”

As Germans tend to be very task-oriented, it is recommended to prepare (especially) well. Know who you will be talking to and what subjects you want to cover. If you promised a product demonstration, make sure all is set accordingly; for example, better inquire in advance whether there is a Wi-Fi-connection for visitors if you want to showcase your SaaS solution. Don’t forget to carry the necessary adapters to plug in your laptop (power sockets are type F, the standard voltage is 230 V, and the standard frequency is 50 Hz). Respect your counterpart’s time schedule—most likely, he or she will have blocked only the amount of time you have agreed upon when you scheduled the appointment.

But, who should you try to schedule the meeting with in the first place? For example, when you want to arrange for a sales meeting, should you contact the specialist buyer (for the items that you offer) or the head of purchasing? I am happy that I had the opportunity to discuss this and some related topics with a proven expert, German Sales Trainer and Business Coach Achim Borse; “There can only be one target person—the decision maker,” was Borse’s answer to this question. In his experience, however, most people would bank on someone in the company who holds a position comparable to their own, someone they consider to be their counterpart on the customer’s side. A field sales professional, for instance, will often contact a buyer at the target company. Why? “Because we are in the habit of doing so,” Borse explained to me. “Habits, however, are not the decisive criteria when choosing a point of entry for prospecting!”

For Borse, “decision maker” is the person with the power to say yes to your proposal; this person presides over the budget and decides how the funds are allocated. He elaborated that decision makers can have different titles and functions; “They do not necessarily have to be on the executive board of a corporation or be the CEO of a firm. What counts is who provides the budget for your proposal.” Who holds this position can vary from company to company; for Borse, it is vital to determine who this person is because “with anybody else you speak to, their decision will depend on the budget; with the decision maker, the budget depends on their decision." So, don't be shy about cold calling someone high(er than you) on the corporate ladder; you can still bring your superior along when you have managed to arrange a meeting.

It cannot be emphasized too often that Germans (overall) are very task-oriented. That concept might be more difficult for you to deal with when you are from a country where people normally put more emphasis on relationships, or where you would assume that things never go as planned anyway. Here, when you request a meeting, let people know what's in it for them. Some time ago, a businessman from Brazil asked me if I could arrange some meetings for him; he was coming to Germany for an exhibition and had researched the names of three university professors in the area. I asked him, "What should the meetings be about?" He told me that he just wanted to visit the lecturers at their faculties. I tried to rephrase my question; "What should I tell them about the purpose of your visit?" His reply was: "Purpose? All I want is to visit them!" OK, another attempt: "What is it you want to discuss with them?" Now Eduardo seemed really frustrated; "I just want to visit them!"

When you ask a (mainstream) German, especially when you have not met him or her before, to dedicate time to talk to you, please keep in mind that, for us, time is a resource. Once a moment is gone, it's gone; it won't come back. Not in this life, and certainly not in another. Normally, we do one thing at a time. We focus and concentrate to get a task done, think about a problem, or enjoy time with our friends and family. When a German agrees to meet you in a business context, please remember that his or her reasoning most probably will be: "I am investing my time; therefore, I want to know what is in it for me." Showing up without an agenda, without having researched the needs of your counterpart, and expecting them to spend some hours with you "just to get to know each other" does hardly work in Germany. In the worst-case scenario, the German will perceive your behavior as unprofessional and disrespectful.

As Syed pointed out, you should book your appointments in time. What "in time" means depends heavily on the industry and the people you want to talk to. Regarding German publishers exhibiting at the *Frankfurter Buchmesse* in October, in my experience, contacting them in

August is a good time. If you look at *analytica* in Munich, the world's largest trade fair for the laboratory technology, analysis, and biotechnology sectors, two months before the show might be far too late; exhibitors in *that* industry at least are used to planning everything well in advance. Executives attending *ISPO MUNICH* or other annual shows might be more flexible and willing to "squeeze you in" on short notice.

When scheduling a business trip, keep in mind that most offices in Germany are either closed during Christmas and New Year (December 24 to January 1) or operate on skeleton staff, and that during the summer, many people are on holiday, sometimes for up to three weeks in a row. Visiting companies during the months of June, July, and August can be a good opportunity to find people in an agreeable, rather relaxed mood; however, there's also a fair chance that half the company will be on holiday, and people will be reluctant to agree to see you because not all relevant colleagues are there to join the meeting. Therefore, better keep yourself informed about public and school holidays in the federal states that you want to visit. And, remember that Saturday is not a working day in Germany; many companies also close early on Fridays. While I, as a freelancer, sometimes meet foreign visitors on a Saturday, only on very rare occasions do I accept any meetings for Sundays. Sunday is sacred to (most) Germans, irrespective of whether or not they go to church. When talking to decision makers in the manufacturing industries or in trade, it may happen that you are offered a meeting as early as 8 a.m.; especially in the manufacturing industry, many are reluctant to miss their (around 10 o'clock) breakfast break. With other industries, you can assume that office hours are generally from nine to five, and that people want to go for lunch sometime between 12 and 1 o'clock.

If you manage to arrange for a meeting at around 11 a.m., you can perhaps suggest having lunch together. If it is your first encounter with the company, or you are in the early stages of your client relationship, you might be invited to join the team at the canteen or for a bite at a down-to-earth restaurant in the neighborhood. If a manager (someone who can probably easily get a refund from Accounting for entertaining visitors) sits at the table, chances are you will be invited. If you can lunch with "only" some of the lower-ranking staff, it would be a nice gesture to ask if you may take care of the bill.

Don't forget to tip five–10 percent; not more, as that might be perceived as pretentious. Waiters receive a (basic) salary and do not live off their tips, as might be the case in your country. If you are using your credit card (which you should not assume is possible everywhere!), you would add the tip amount when signing the slip or leave some silver coins on the table. If you pay cash, just tell the waiter or waitress to round it up. For example, when the bill sums up to 46 euros and the service was okay, tell the waiter, "50, please." If in doubt, and your guests already know what you will pay, you can always ask them what they recommend as an appropriate tip. By the way, in Germany, it is common to also tip cab drivers and bartenders, and most of the time, people would also leave a small coin or two (maybe 50 eurocents) for the janitor or cleaning staff at a public convenience or restaurant toilet.

When arranging your meetings, consider using all available channels such as the telephone, e-mail, matchmaking tools (as often offered for trade shows), and social media. However, take care that your approach complies with the General Data Protection Regulation (GDPR), a directive that requires businesses to protect the personal data and privacy of EU citizens for transactions that occur within EU member states. Make sure people can research you and your enterprise to double-check who is contacting them. Be present and active on LinkedIn and maybe even XING, the German pendant. Publish a professional portrait as your profile picture—sunglasses and scanned passport pictures are taboo! And don't forget to keep your website up to date.

Make your written communication personal (if possible, address the recipient by name) and individual (do not suppose that "one template fits all"). Give your e-mail a meaningful subject line and always mention the purpose of your attempt to get in touch; for example, what is the intended result of a meeting? Try to be very clear and to the point. Unless you (already) know the person, write in a matter-of-fact, formal style (not flowery and prose-y). Submit flawless sales collaterals that are well structured; do not attach eight MB presentations or 20 product pictures. Put the most important keywords at the beginning of the subject line, as you don't know how many characters will be displayed in the preview of the recipient's e-mail program.

It never leaves a good impression if one can see that a lot of copy and pasting has been done. When you compile your e-mail by recycling old messages, first copy the text fragments into a .txt file, and from there, transfer the result into your mail program so that only one font is used. Avoid exclamation marks and smileys; place emphasis on orthography and punctuation.

Keep it short and avoid pointing out the obvious or coming across as superficial. Try to put yourself in your recipient's shoes and see whether he or she is likely to think "so what?!" after reading a few lines of your message. Take this, for example, "With a huge production capacity at an attractive price, we assure our clients of our best services." So what?! Better: "I have gone through your website and, from what I can see, you must be purchasing a substantial number of xyz items per year. Making no compromises on quality, we have recently developed a product that is 5 percent less costly than the average product available in the market and offers some added benefits such as … We would like to introduce the xyz component and explain its advantages to you or one of your colleagues who will be present at *Anuga* in Cologne next month."

Even if you want to introduce your range of products and services, do not copy and paste your entire portfolio; rather, try to very briefly explain what your key competencies are or what specific topics you would like to discuss. Don't present yourselves as "the leading company" unless you are from Alibaba Group, Gazprom, or maybe Coca-Cola. For a German, who is not used to these kinds of hollow superlatives (as we most probably would perceive them), this claim will instantly undermine your credibility.

When you give someone a call, try to explain who you are very briefly (in the sense, what your company is offering that you assume your contact might need). "This is Robin! I am calling from Abu Dhabi!" is not a suitable introduction. Also, do not repeatedly say "Hello, hello…" when the other person picks up. Some of my Indian clients have that habit, and I would assume that I am not the only one to find it very confusing because, in Germany, nobody does that. It's better to say "can you hear me?" if the connection is bad. When Germans pick up the phone, they usually answer by stating their last name, and if at work, the company name. When I call someone, I would typically say, "Good morning / good afternoon, this is Andra Riemhofer from so-and-so company." Speak slowly, try to avoid an accent, and listen carefully. A German would often find background sounds like street noise or loud chatter annoying; try to shut out any such disturbing commotion.

After the phone call, it can be a good idea to send a follow-up e-mail, confirming the time and place of your meeting, for example. On this occasion, you can share your mobile number, for any eventuality ("Für alle Fälle"). Be careful when sending invitations from Outlook, and so on—the time difference might mess up your schedule; make sure there is no confusion about the day you want to visit. Better confirm "October 11" than, for example, 10/11, because Germans are used to first mentioning the day and then the month (11.10.), and could mistakenly expect you only on November 10. And, since we are on the topic, Germans do not use the a.m./p.m. system; better add "in the morning," "in the afternoon," or "in the evening" when telling time.

Consider hiring a local person to help you with research and setting up appointments; my experience is that Germans are more likely to get involved in a brief conversation if they are called from a local number and if the person calling knows the language and business culture. Recently, having me on board for meetings with German contacts tremendously helped a delegation from Finland to confirm (more) meetings. Without the prospect of a German-speaking person to "jump in" in case of (potential) language difficulties, some contacts had initially refused to agree to meet the foreign visitors. Also, please remember that, in Germany, we don't have this habit of re-confirming the meeting one or two days in advance (unless that procedure is specifically agreed upon, or maybe a strike, volcanic eruption, or blizzard has challenged your travel plans). I tend to recommend to my clients that it is better *not* to re-confirm. Firstly, it could confuse people, and secondly, your prospect might take the opportunity to cancel the meeting at short notice (for example, if something of higher priority has come up in the meantime).

What else should you consider when traveling to Germany for doing business? Senior Business Development Manager Stephan Janouch drew my attention to the fact that, although most Germans should know enough English to provide directions or engage in a short conversation, and while comprehension of the English language might be above average on a global scale (particularly within companies that are conducting business internationally), there are two things that are ignored quite frequently: firstly, he highlights what you can subsume under the heading reading is not talking. "A lot of people do have an excellent English vocabulary and understanding of the English language, but feel uncomfortable when they are forced to engage in a live conversation," he explains. "In many cases, this results from a lack of practice." As an example, he mentions the average engineer who is used to reading datasheets, specifications, or conference papers, which are typically available only in English. "He or she may not have issues verbalizing facts in written form but could easily find it challenging when asked to do real-time interpreting," Janouch warns.

I can *totally* relate to what he is saying. I did my A-levels in English and German (at the time, we had to major in two subjects), and during my undergraduate studies, scored high in the written Business English tests. I was not very used to speaking English, because at school and in higher education, little emphasis is put on oral communication. When I, at the age of 25, went to India for an internship, and my family there recommended that I should call the managing director to confirm that I would actually show up on October 1 (my flight had been scheduled for only a few days after 9/11, so the request made sense to me), I postponed the call *for days*; I was so afraid the publisher would instantly send me back when he heard my bad English! So, don't be surprised to maybe find the person you have been communicating with easily via e-mail being comparatively sparing with words when you finally meet him or her face-to-face.

Secondly, the business development manager points out that, in many cases, the vocabulary of German English speakers is limited to two categories—the basic set of words, grammar, and semantics you learn in school and the specialized terminology according to one's profession. Between these usually lies a gap that contains a lot of the subtleties and idioms of English language which may result in a misunderstanding (bad) or miscommunication (dangerous). One should bear in mind that, although both languages are similar in many ways, there are words a typical German would have difficulty understanding (e.g., the term "evangelizing"). There are words with a completely unrelated translation—a German would be able to relate to roentgen rays (Röntgenstrahlen) but maybe not to X-rays—and there are similar sounding words with a completely different meaning. Take, for example, the German word "eventuell," which should be translated as "possibly," rather than "eventually;" a German could easily decode a "we will eventually reach a conclusion" as "we will *maybe* reach a conclusion." I remember how I, as a 12-year-old, told my English teacher's mom (an elderly lady from Great Britain) that I was afraid to meet her; "afraid" just sounded so similar to the very polite "erfreut" (pleased, delighted).

Today, I sometimes still get confused by "you must not," which if you translate it into German word by word, means that you don't *need* to (do something). If a German tells you that you must *not* do something, and you wonder how this could make sense (e.g., "you must not reconfirm our meeting"), better ask him or her to explain or rephrase. Janouch highly recommends understanding how proficient your counterpart is in speaking English and adapt accordingly.

During the meeting, stay matter-of-fact, stick to the agreed agenda, and at the end, (try to) conclude any talks or agreement with a wrap-up. Largely lacking a "hands on, can do" mentality, Germans are (otherwise) sometimes easily tempted to postpone decisions, wishing to (again) review certain aspects of a matter and discuss them at length with xyz party. A wrap-up that you can, for example, title "Next Steps" can help speed things up a bit. Choose your words carefully so that you are not perceived as pushy. Offer to compile a written protocol and ask who you should e-mail it to (preferably the decision maker).

What to Consider for Face-to-Face Presentations and Online Meetings

When you finally sit at the table, let your counterpart also talk, even if he or she is not as fluent as you would have hoped for! No matter how much time you have spent preparing the perfect sales pitch, if you do not let the other person participate in the conversation, he or she might feel frustrated and chances are you will never find out exactly what they need.

When asked for the best possible (sales) strategy, Achim Borse replied: "The one, sacred approach doesn't exist. However, all prospecting approaches should share a common structure." His main piece of advice: "Stop selling—in the sense of overselling—and you'll be instantly more successful." He explained to me that, when you talk too much in the opening stages of a conversation, without putting forth questions to the customers, without engaging them actively in the exchange, and without allowing them to talk, and not (properly) listening to them, you'll be giving them the impression that you are trying to con them into a purchase. "And that is what people nowadays can't stand anymore," he concluded. "We are dealing with self-confident, autonomous customers." His advice: "Start replacing your statements with questions. Masters of prospecting are masters at asking questions—not at argumentation." So, before you start presenting your solution, don't forget to (first) inquire about your prospective clients' need(s); you can try to refer to your audiences' specific problems when delivering the presentation.

My cousin Arjun Sachdev, whose company represents German publishers looking to sell their online databases in India, has observed that "in most cases, Germans, in terms of business, are very to-the-point and upfront." Apart from them normally not being very warm in terms of business dealings (as compared to people in India, for example), he has experienced that, in a business context "Germans prefer to hear the practical opportunity rather than the ideal opportunity." You should "hence, always be honest and back your talk with facts and figures."

Yes, I would agree with that. Always keep in mind that problem-focused Germans are eager to hear about concrete solutions (rather than visionary ideas that we would most readily label "dream castles"). Therefore, you should highlight your expertise in solving problems and try to give examples, and mention references. I recommend that, when you talk about reference clients, instead of (or maybe in addition to) displaying the logos of the usual suspects in your presentation (depending on your industry, these can be big market players such as BMW, SAP, or Springer-Verlag), you should talk about how you have helped specialized businesses of comparable size (to your target client) solve specific problems. However, don't forget to ask your reference customer(s) for permission first! And, be prepared to be told that your target clients' problems are not at all comparable, or at least, are *much* more complex and challenging.

It can be a good idea to position yourself as a consultant (who helps solve problems), rather than to present yourself as a service provider:

looking at cross-cultural communication and its potential pitfalls, John Otto Magee, an independent consultant who advises global companies on cross-border collaborations, has observed that "Germans respond positively to American customer-orientation. But that friendliness and responsiveness must be backed up by a solution to a problem." He, in his article *Business Mentality: Germans Consult, Americans Serve,* advises that, when dealing with Germans, one should avoid the terms "serve" and "service" at first, and talk about "consulting" instead. "German customers might hear 'serve' as a substitute for real and proven knowledge and expertise." In his article, which mainly targets business people from the United States, he concludes that one should also "try [to] stay detached and even distant from the customer as a person, to depersonalize the relationship and remain an outsider lending his expertise to a specific problem." As an American (however, that could apply to people from many other countries, as well), one "should delve earlier than [your] instincts suggest into the complex and critical issues and start asking penetrating questions right away." Magee warns that "[o]therwise the Germans will think [you] either do not grasp problems in their complexity or do not dare to address them" (Magee 2018a).

Present yourself as competent, knowledgeable, and open. As a thumb rule, your presentation should be well structured and factual, with well-documented sources, and not have too much "blah blah;" that means avoid superfluous talk and try to get to the point quickly.

Very often, it is recommendable to add a conclusive summary and suggest next steps/present an action plan. It would be better not to place too much emphasis on humor, as is sometimes the case with Anglo-Saxon presentations. If you present in English, and there is no simultaneous translation, speak slowly and clearly, without too much of an accent. (Some) jokes or allegories might not translate; for the same reason, be careful when using idioms and sports phrases. For example, do not expect us to know what a ballpark figure is, or what it means to be far out in left field. Be clear up-front about how you want to run the presentation and make well-defined recommendations, but at the same time, give space for discussion at the end. "Don't be afraid of having a contrary view to seniors or the majority," Manoj Barve from India adds, "so long as you can defend it. And, no 'thank you' slide, please!" Thank you, Manoj!

When a German asks a question, try to give an answer. If you have not understood the question (or find it stupid), do not evade the question or change the subject. It's better to ask the other person to kindly rephrase the question. If you're still in doubt regarding what he or she is unclear about, you can say, "That is indeed an interesting question." Pause and look as if you are contemplating your answer. Germans are not used to this kind of silence and chances are you will get more input. You can always proceed with "if I got you right, you are saying that …" or "In my experience ...," and see whether you're heading in the right direction. If you (still) cannot answer the question, tell the enquirer that you honestly don't know, but that you will find out and get back to him or her later (don't forget to actually do that!). A German will most likely be satisfied with that answer.

Considering the style of presentation, I am hesitant to tell you what the best possible solution is; I honestly doubt there is *one* best way. However, I would suggest that a good approach is to keep in mind the core values and practices introduced in this text (such as Germans' task orientation, sticking to an agenda and timeline, not getting too emotional, and so on), while at the same time, not denying yourself. Maybe your way of mixing facts and figures with a good storyline and your unique way of talking to an audience will be perceived as exceptionally refreshing and engaging. Professor for International Management Daniel Ittstein has observed that the presentation style in Germany has (anyway) changed fundamentally over the last five years. He recommends concentrating on a good storyline and being visual and authentic.

A good storyline, at least for me, can still be on how you were challenged by a problem, how you maybe struggled at first to find a solution, and then how you finally came up with what you present today. Because, in Germany, we do not particularly believe in superheroes, it (generally) couldn't harm to talk not only about strengths, but also about weaknesses; sharing insights about how you (initially) struggled or failed will emphasize the complexity of the problem and make you more credible and trustworthy.

While you should consider the use of other/additional media, apart from PowerPoint or Flipchart, I recommend that you think twice before playing your five- to seven-minute corporate video, even if watching the film makes your own heart beat faster. You are here to discuss business and get to know the other person(s). If the video helps to explain certain concepts or capacities, know which part of the film you need to play to make your point; if the spectator senses that watching the film will hardly promote findings—and the time could be otherwise used more profitably—he or she might feel annoyed.

Try to engage the audience. As an icebreaker, you could, for example, ask your listeners to assess something; that can be a year (when something was invented) or you can let them guess the number of xyz items that are sold in your home market in an average year. I once listened to a German publishing professional who, at a conference, shared her story of how she had reinvented schoolbooks for gardening apprentices; as an introduction to her presentation, she asked the audience to close their eyes and imagine they were members of her target group. In an almost hypnotic tone, she went on to tell us that we were 15 years old and had just left school with not-so-good marks … While initially feeling slightly uncomfortable, I quickly got hooked by her presentation. However, be careful to not surprise your audience too much or bring them too far beyond their comfort zone.

When you showcase the features of a software program or SaaS solution, you can ask the audience what tasks you should execute first; for example, let them decide whether you should run a search by "x" or "y" parameters, or ask them the criteria according to which you should sort/compile the data. Under no circumstances should you just reel off your demonstration.

Be careful how you comment on your audiences' contributions, and make sure you don't come off as being superficial or patronizing. "A big round of applause for Ms. Meier for knowing the year of the French Revolution" might make Ms. Meier feel as if she is in kindergarten again! This reminds me of an episode Consultant Alexander Wurz shared with me; when all the Germans, at the end of a presentation, knocked on the tables (which means "thank you for the presentation"), and the French speaker was so irritated and shocked that he left the room; he perceived the knocking as a very negative sign.

Wurz recommended that I should, when talking about presentations, also mention the relevance of the untranslatable German word "nachvollziehen." The term means a lot more than just "understanding" (what you are saying). Your (German) audience should always be able to "nachvollziehen" your line of thought, that is, comprehend where you are coming from and how you reached your conclusion(s)—what data you are relating to, what thoughts you had, maybe what pros and cons you weighed, which sources you used, what the (possible) consequences are (e.g., of implementing a solution)—so that the listeners can integrate/bring your idea in line with what they already know / their world view / their specific challenges. Be prepared to be asked how you reached your conclusion/solution, and don't respond to the question with a "Why are you bothered? Just be happy it works!" attitude.

"Expect to be challenged," Sue De'Ath warns, and "don't wing it," as a German business professional working in the United States admonishes. "Germans have a comparably long attention span," adds a German who currently lives and works in the United Kingdom; according to him, we can easily digest (aren't we rather hungry for?) lots of facts and figures. Be prepared to be confronted with all possible questions. "Der Teufel steckt im Detail" (the devil is in the details), a German would typically comment, when he or she is under the impression that something has not been thoroughly thought through. Germans almost unconsciously examine things for hidden problems; planning must consider all eventualities.

Ruben A. Hernandez, in his book *Presenting Across Cultures*, explains:

> *Germans will also listen critically, scanning your talk for inconsistencies and errors or for exceptions to any claim you may make. They generally feel uncomfortable with partial truths, believing that, if something is not 100 percent true, then it cannot be true at all. (Hernandez 2013, p. 75)*

If any inconsistency or inaccuracies are perceived, be prepared for them to be pointed out. I once feared running into a major credibility problem when I was presenting the results of an advertising copy test; one of the engineers who had joined my client's marketing team seriously confronted me with the question of how the results of our survey could be trusted when we, as a publishing house, could not even master punctuation rules (a comma was missing in the introduction!). The head of marketing was signaling to me that everything was under control, rolling her eyes heavenward … however, knowing that I had at least one listener who would not mind spoiling my presentation by highlighting even minor flaws made the experience less than enjoyable.

Magee explains that Germans tend to separate message from messenger: "A German presenter consciously moves into the background so that the content can take center stage." According to common (German) understanding, arguments should speak for themselves. "German speakers strive to be factual, analytical, scientific," Magee elaborates. "This often makes them appear objective, impersonal, and colorless. They display little body language and stay behind the podium or to the side. Content takes center stage." In his experience, Americans do the opposite: "They link message and messenger." Content, form, and presenter should form a unity: "Sell yourself first, then your product or service." So, Americans get personal and anecdotal, with personal color and plenty of gesticulation. For those not familiar with this style, he recommends going to YouTube and studying Steve Ballmer on stage in his Microsoft days. Well, *that* style, at least to me, feels somewhat odd indeed, and I didn't watch *only* the "going crazy on stage" clip. Obviously, I am not alone: Germans, Magee explains, react ambivalently to this linking of message and messenger: "While listening, they whisper to each other: 'If his case is so strong, why is he putting on such a ridiculous show?' or 'Typical American. All show, no substance. We'll take him down when we get to Q&A.'" Yet, some of the Germans, according to Magee, "secretly think: 'Wow. Uninhibited. Natural. Believes in himself. Getting me to believe. Wish we Germans were allowed to do the same'" (Magee 2018b).

Well, even when I have said before that you should not deny yourself, I would still recommend trying to follow a slightly more "conservative" approach (as compared to Ballmer), and for the occasion, to dress (more) formally. Depending on the industry, I would prefer to see you wear a jacket, if not a tie as well. As we are on the topic of appearance: if you are used to carrying a rucksack, please double-check that it is still in good shape. Leather bags may have *some* patina, while shoes really should not reveal their advanced age! Avoid extensive use of aftershave and (no offence) make sure your clothes do not smell of naphthalene. Women should also use only discreet perfumes, and avoid flashy makeup and jewelry. Business women over here generally prefer to "dress down" and would rarely wear high-heeled stilettos or figure-accentuating (short) outfits. Men are used to seeing their female colleagues in trouser suits or knee-length pencil skirts. I am not telling you that, as a woman, you should mimic the local, more "functional" style; however, you must consider that a very feminine outfit might lead to your potential (German) business partner perceiving you as less professional than you actually are. But, if being underestimated is your preferred strategy, ignore what I have just said.

When adapting presentations and sales collaterals to the German market, pick your language provider carefully, and under no circumstances, use Google Translate. Also, it would be better not to blindly trust a local language provider who says that he or she is working with a German native. And, do not let anybody who is not familiar with the industry translate your spec sheets and brochures. It would be useful to keep in mind that translations from English to German, as a thumb rule, require 1.3 times more space than the original text. Adapt the metrics (e.g., square meters instead of square feet) and preferably convert prices into euros. Keep in mind that most people in Europe may have never heard of "crore" and "lakh," and might find it difficult to think in terms of gallons, yards, or inches.

When designing your PowerPoint presentation or sales collaterals, do not use meaningless icons or low-resolution pictures, and consider cutting down on flashy colors. Use good-quality paper for your brochures and focus on the message you want to convey. Be careful with green letters on a red background or vice versa (I have seen that!); about 8 percent of men are red–green color blind in one way or another.

If, at a trade fair, your goal is to present new products, the attention needs to be directed to the products. You need to display the items in an attractive and prominent way and highlight the product's advantages. Shipping the goods back and forth might be expensive, but only displaying a poster of what you intend to sell won't do the job. What you *can* showcase on a poster are product specifications and advantages. Don't forget that, if you are not yet renowned in the market, you very often first need to convince people that the items on display are more than just cheap copies. A friend of mine purchases electromechanical components; he says that, for him, it is crucial that he can weigh the parts he is considering in his hands … to be able to touch and feel the goods. You should be prepared to answer his detailed questions to his full satisfaction. Like most Germans, he would expect to communicate with international exhibitors in English.

What else should you keep in mind when meeting Germans face-to-face? Be aware that cross-cultural body language can easily be misinterpreted; so, if you feel like the person listening to you looks confused, you can try meta-communication. For example, you can say: "You don't seem to agree? Please tell me if I said or did something to confuse you."

Also, keep in mind that Germans generally prefer a bit more personal space than people in South America or Greece, for example. When the German at your table readjusts his or her chair during your product demonstration, moving it a bit farther afield from where you are sitting, do not try to regain proximity; your listener—being used to keeping others at a greater distance—might start feeling very uncomfortable. If you are from the United States, you might experience just the opposite and feel that Germans come way too close. Better avoid touching the other person's arm or other parts of the body when talking. Don't slap a German on the shoulder unless you already know him very well. When it comes to women, avoid this habit completely.

When you meet people (only) virtually, the challenges can be of a different nature, and one could write a separate book on *that* topic alone. Munich-based Trainer Gudrun Höhne, an expert in the fields of global communication and virtual teams, currently authors such a guidebook and allowed me a sneak preview of her manuscript. Here are some basic principles that she advises you should follow:

Her first (standard) piece of advice concerns the technical part of the communication via Skype, WebEx, and comparable solutions. If you have received a meeting link from your (German) business partner, better check the link beforehand and make sure that your firewall settings do not generate any technical problems. While such technical pitfalls can always happen, I would assume that Germans are generally less tolerant of those not having taken standard precautions. If, however, *you* send the meeting link, make sure that an agenda is attached to your invitation, and inform the recipients of how they can check the technical settings. If the scheduled timeslot allows for some buffer, you may mention in the agenda that, according to your planning, the presentation should (as an example) take half an hour, and that another 15 minutes are allocated for Q&A.

Check the position of your webcam before going online, and make sure that you have a professional, neutral background. I remember the embarrassment I felt during a Skype job interview some years ago, and how I tried to discreetly move my laptop so that the other person wouldn't see bits of the ironing board stored behind a closet at my back. Höhne advises that you should dress professionally, as for a normal business meeting or presentation, and avoid wearing shirts with small patterns because this consumes too much Internet bandwidth.

You should take care that you are in a quiet environment, and that there are no disturbances; close the windows and doors, mute your phone, and redirect incoming calls to voicemail. According to her recommendations, you should also double-check that you have a stable Internet connection. Join the meeting at least five minutes before the official start to ensure everything is set up correctly.

"Germans expect you to be in the meeting on time," Höhne points out. "Start with small talk but keep it a bit shorter than usual because Germans like to focus on the subject at hand." She also suggests that you talk slowly and clearly, avoid slang, and unless you can converse in German, keep in mind that you are not talking to native speakers.

When sharing your screen, and before you proceed with your demonstration, you should ask your audience whether they can see whatever you want them to see (only that and not more); allow for a time delay. It is recommendable to summarize and visualize important points (you can use the service's whiteboard feature, for example), and ask for comments and feedback to check your audiences' understanding. With larger groups, it is best to have a co-moderator and also use the chat for communication in the meeting.

Let me close by sharing a story one of my German friends related to me when we were discussing international calls: where he works, there is a regular (like weekly or monthly) online meeting with colleagues and representatives working in the United States. Obviously, he explained, the meetings are always held in English. "One day, but only after 10–15 minutes, we realized that actually, no American was present in the call. We could easily have held the meeting in German." However, my friend continued, "the managing director, who was in his flow and couldn't easily adapt to new circumstances, stuck to his procedure and continued in his (improvable) English, going through the meeting points exactly as they were listed on his paper." Don't tell me I haven't warned you enough …

RFPs, Quotes, and Negotiations: How to Close the Deal with Germans

When it comes to discussing definite business opportunities, how you want to handle the situation will depend on your branch of trade and the common (international) business practices in your industry. The way in which tenders are prepared and contracts are awarded in the insurance industry may differ from the way they are handled in the construction or fast-moving consumer goods industries; the terms of payment you can negotiate may depend not only on your company's credit rating, but also on the economic strength and political stability of your home country. What I can offer you are some basic principles that should help you to put yourself in a good position, no matter what the specific opportunity is.

Regardless of whether you send or receive a request for proposal (RFP), use the occasion to (again) establish yourself as serious and trustworthy ("in German terms"), and keep in mind that your client or supplier would want to use their time effectively (how Germans generally consider "time" has been explained in Chapter 5).

When submitting a request for quotation (RFQ), make sure to send all the required information and leave as little room for queries as possible; however, highlight the areas in which you want your supplier to make suggestions. Don't let your enquiry look like a bulk mail unless you operate in a distinct buyers' market. In some cases, it can be a good idea to give a (reasonable!) target price. Formal and polite communication will help you build a rapport. If people enjoy communicating with you, they are more likely to go the extra mile. If demand is higher than supply, being agreeable and reliable ("zuverlässig") will help you tap and nurture sources.

When receiving an inquiry, you can briefly confirm receipt and let the sender know by when he or she can expect your quotation. Calling the sender to double-check on certain positions in the RFQ can be a good idea (to also give your business relationship a more personal touch);

however, do not ask nonsense questions. If you cannot meet the deadline mentioned in the inquiry, ask your (potential) client whether they can extend it to a certain time.

Throughout my career, both as an employed sales person and now as a freelancer, I have had good experiences with being transparent with my German clients: When I know that I can't meet a deadline or target price, or cannot submit a quote for other reasons, I let the other person know. Some years ago, when I was representing a company from the Gulf region, we received an invitation to quote for a *very* attractive, high-volume project that put dollar signs in our eyes. Our German prospect was a re-seller, meaning, he needed *our* quote to calculate and submit a quote to *his* client. Looking at the technical specifications of the discussed project and the special strengths and matching capacities of the supplier I was representing, everything looked good; however, knowing that the ultimate buyer would want us to handle material displaying pictures of scantily clad (to say the least) women, I advised the Gulf company to first double-check the feasibility of the proposed project. "No problem, we surely can handle the job," was their initial answer. "Don't worry," was the second reply. "Let us first win the project, and then we'll figure it all out," I was told when I still insisted (eager not to put *my* reputation at risk). Only after I had asked the German prospect to send some sample images taken from a former project did we discover that, under my client's country's legislation, it was *prohibited (!)* to do such a job and that we could never have fulfilled the order. Imagine the situation, had the German prospect been awarded the project based on our pricing! The German client was disappointed about the fact that we couldn't quote, but *very* much appreciated us being transparent on the matter. We soon got another chance from him!

There is another lesson to learn from this story: Don't say "no problem" to a German if there *is* a problem, because when *we* answer a question with "no problem!," we most probably mean "no problem!" As outlined in Chapter 4, Germans tend to take words literally and are not well trained in reading between the lines or understanding vague hints.

For example, many Germans who have not yet spoken much to business contacts from India will take a "no problem" from them literally. "Can we get a 50 percent discount?"—"No problem (we will deduct

50 percent);" "Will you be visiting Germany again soon?"—"No problem (we can shortly fix a meeting)." For those who have already done business in India, the "no problem"—I sadly must say—is a big red rag. Very often, Germans would have taken their business partners literally, and are now convinced that Indians promise everything under the sun and are not reliable at all. Better replace "no problem" with "I see," "uh huh," or "interesting," and when there *is* a problem, just tell us!

When you receive the first RFQ from a potential buyer, don't get too excited; Germans are not exactly famous for making quick decisions. Very often, they are interested in identifying a second source, but will only buy from you (for the first time) when their current supplier lets them down. Letting you quote could be a means of getting to know you better, just in case! Keep that in mind while you do your best to leave a good (first) impression. Very often, you would initially be awarded only a smaller project, which, in my experience, is a very good starting point. If you handle the small job properly, bigger ones may follow. I mention that because my international clients sometimes seem disappointed when I proudly present an initial RFQ that does not exactly match their stretched goals in terms of sales volume.

You can easily spoil the deal at the very early stages by disregarding some details that might not seem especially important to *you*, but are crucial when it comes to what Germans generally consider proper business practices. Call us "picky," but when we receive an e-mail, PDF-quote, or other business communication displaying a pixelated company logo, we can quickly conclude that the sender is somewhat sloppy in everything he or she does, including fulfilling our order. If you use a predefined form to submit your quote, and there is blank space captioned "company name," put the recipient's address in it; do not write "miscellaneous."

Make sure you get the names right (if your keyboard doesn't offer a "ü," then address Mr. Müller as Mr. Mueller; same with "ä"—"ae," "ö"—"oe," and "ß"—"ss"). Also, take care to get the spaces (e.g., *after* the punctuation) right. I don't think great harm is done if you mistakenly address Thomas Müller as Mr. Thomas; however, as a thumb rule, try to remember that the last (mentioned) name is the family name and that you address people with the formal "Mr." or "Ms." and add that last name (unless you are already on a first-name basis).

In case you are in doubt about certain specifications in the inquiry, it's better to double-check, rather than just quote something. If you cannot comply with some requirements, and would like to offer an (in *your* eyes, at least) even better alternative, highlight the parts where your quote does not match the requirements. Do not let things go unmentioned; if the RFQ reads "shrink wrapped" and you lack the machine, do not just leave out the wrapping and packing part.

All documents must appear well structured, so if your proposal consists of more than one or two pages, it is a good idea to paginate them. When submitting several documents, help the receiver sort them out by attaching an index of what is what. Conclude the quote by inviting the receiver to respond to you in case there are questions, and display your contact details visibly. "Hope the above is clear and of interest for you. Looking forward to hear from you" (as copied from a proposal I once reviewed) might come across as too casual, if not outright sloppy.

Be careful with abbreviations (unless they're very common ones in international trade and your respective industry) and provide a deadline until when the quote is valid. You can also use that to speed things up a bit and put gentle pressure on your (prospective) client.

I advise my clients to submit their quotes as PDF attachments preferably; this way, the recipient can easily print and forward the document, and the formatting will not get messed up. Better make sure that whatever digital documents you submit, they do not vary too much from our standard letter-format DIN A4 (210 × 297 mm). To learn more about common norms and standards, please refer to the website of the German Institute for Standardization (www.din.de/en).

Even with small things (as outlined), leave no room for doubt that one can rely on you 100 percent. Germans tend to consider each and every decision very carefully; do not expect them to act spontaneously or "just try something out." Many a time, you need a lot of staying power if you want to gain a presence in the market. Even if they do not buy from you now, keep in touch and try to meet them at the next industry event or during a business trip. Invite them to your offices, write a Christmas card, ask them whether they want to receive your newsletter, and keep them updated about new products and special offers; but under no circumstances should you spam their inbox by repeatedly sending follow-up mails.

Always keep in mind that Germans, in general terms, are very process-oriented and risk-averse. I once had a client from the United States who found it hard to digest that she, during the initial stages of discussion with a German head of marketing regarding a potential collaboration, was confronted with questions like: "Suppose we decide to work together, let us assume that, in two years, our company gets taken over; how would that event affect § 4.2 of our agreement?" My client made several attempts to explain that one should get started on working together and need not be concerned about eventualities before they materialize. Even if you feel annoyed by such an infatuation with detail, or in case you do not have an answer to that question, keep in mind that Germans are truly concerned with many eventualities that, in their thinking, might need to be considered. Don't give us the feeling that you don't care about our concerns. The point mentioned might turn out to be totally irrelevant (even to the German), but showing us that you (also) care will earn you many brownie points. "Good point, we will double-check with the legal department; however, that might take some time," was what I said.

When a German is ready to take your business relationship to the next level, he or she will most likely explicitly tell you and expects the same from you. Some years ago, I supported a Swedish company exhibiting their machines at a trade show. Upfront, the managing director had briefed me about the three most important German target customers. Already being aware that our Nordic neighbors sometimes come across as even less emotional than we (watch the Danish crime show *Forbrydelsen*, and in contrast, any episode of the German *Tatort* will feel like Italian opera), I wasn't surprised to see my client with what I (still) thought was supposed to be a poker face when one of the prospects showed up. Both gentlemen engaged (in fluent English) in discussing a business opportunity, including what steps to take next. In the meanwhile, I attended to other visitors, and having watched the greater part of the talk from a distance, it looked to me as if the German appeared somehow unsatisfied when he left. I asked the exhibitor whether there had been any problems and if anything did not go as expected. The Swede seemed puzzled, "Why? It looks like he'll be buying, doesn't it?" The funny thing was that, after a few minutes, the German returned and explicitly (also) asked whether he had missed something, if everything was alright, and if he could (still) expect to receive whatever my client had held out in prospect.

Germans tend to need clarity, be it (about) a "yes" or "no." Business Consultant John Otto Magee, in his article *Lost in Translation—German Directness, American Euphemisms: The Hell of Cross-Cultural Communication,* explains what can happen when a German doesn't get a "no," and what can cause such a situation in the first place:

> *[T]he American no comes in the form of a conditional yes signaling the reasons why assistance is regretfully not possible. To Americans it is a sign of professionalism and finesse to communicate rejection in a positive, supportive, affirmative way. This is not easy for Germans to decipher. Germans want clarity. But a no in the form of a conditional yes sends mixed signals.*
>
> *The resulting misunderstandings can get ugly. Germans may think they have an agreement, whereas the Americans communicated no such thing. Germans will then conclude that the Americans are unzuverlässig (unreliable). Even on minor matters, to be unzuverlässig is a character flaw in Germany. Unzuverlässig is a label which can take a painfully long time to have peeled off your forehead. (Magee 2018b)*

When discussing a deal with Germans, make an effort to be as transparent and unambiguous as possible (although I don't mean that you should put *all* your cards on the table). First, establish what the subject and objective of the negotiations are. Ensure that your counterpart is the right person, with the authority to make a deal. If things are complex, agree on the procedure first before you address the subject matter; an agreement on procedures can be confidence-building and facilitate the subsequent negotiations.

A marketing executive from France told me that, when dealing with Germans, she prepares the negotiation in the same way as with persons from other countries, "except that I give more explanations and background information. I do the small talk *after* the negotiation and, with other nations, *before* the negotiation; I don't add emotional components in the negotiations."

Germans tend to prepare themselves to the smallest detail before a negotiation or a conversation, and expect the same from others. They will take their time to analyze each and every aspect of a decision before they agree to something. It is considered a good idea to gather a lot of background information, including on your prospective business partner. In Achim Borse's experience (he coaches companies on these matters), negotiations are then conducted quickly, fairly, and without detours. "Unforeseen last-minute changes are not welcome," he says.

Senior Project Manager Hasan Syed advises that you should talk about the advantages and disadvantages (of a proposal) as you would list them in bullet points on paper. "Be straightforward and discuss the limitations of the current offer. If you have a real, viable reason for why it needs to be negotiated up or down, it will happen," he says.

Almost all parties I interviewed mentioned that you should not get emotional, stay factual and to-the-point, and that you shouldn't offer irrelevant information. Be prepared to hear an explicit "no," but don't take it personally. The Germans at the table would share a common understanding that you negotiate about a matter, and that it's not about people or relationships. We tend to quite clearly separate those spheres. "Be prepared, know your numbers, focus on interests," as Professor for International Management Daniel Ittstein would summarize.

Be clear about the transactional value and stick to it. Don't start with a too high and unrealistic price because this is seen as unprofessional and unfair. Germans don't like a carpet market approach and show respect for their partners in the negotiations with a fair deal. "They usually have one goal with perhaps, at maximum, one alternative, and they go for this goal and nothing else," the German CEO of a company located in India explained to me. "So there is no fooling around." According to the C-level executive, trying to find alternatives that aren't exactly matching the Germans' expectations are often considered a waste of time. "Germans want to have exactly *this* for *that* price and want to know by *when* they can get it. Right on the money," he said.

If, on the other hand, you make yourself understood that this is it, and if you are determined about *your* position, you can also leave an impression, he explains. "I am not too sure if our way of doing things is well received in countries where there is more room for negotiation, and where, by cultural background, the parties enjoy bargaining," he adds. "For Germans, it's often just a waste of time to negotiate from 100 to 20; they prefer to start at 30 or 25 to negotiate to the final price of 20." Not every German is as reflective; Intercultural Leadership Trainer Andreas Hauser, on another occasion, commented on how "Germans are often quite convinced that their way is the correct, and sometimes only, way forward to deal with an issue or solve a matter." It might be helpful for you to keep that in mind when you would (normally) expect more flexibility from the person you are dealing with.

Last, but not least, travel author Cal O Cal warns that you will be expected to have all the answers. "Germans are very security-conscious people. They need to have all the boxes checked before committing to anything. Be precise. 1.99 US dollars in Germany is 1.99 US dollars, not 1.99 US dollars plus other things." After all, Borse would add, "for Germans, a contract is 'law.' As it is in the contract, it is implemented. Therefore, from a German point of view, all details must be clarified before signing the contract." Do not (try to) renegotiate on already agreed terms, and keep your side of the bargain!

Do I have any tips on how to make a German move a little bit? Try being silent. Silence is often perceived as very unpleasant, and it is likely that the other party will start making concessions just to change the situation. But *psst!* Don't tell anybody *I* told you so.

CHAPTER 7

How to Maintain (Cordial) Business Relationships

What the Average German Understands by "Good" Relationship

When you work with Germans, you can assume that, basically, you won't hear much from them unless there is (additional) work to discuss, details to be checked, or there is a problem. Don't expect us to give you a casual call from time to time to just check how things (or you) are. Even as vendors, if we follow the same approach that we would apply in Germany, we take care to have a conversational gambit at hand when we call—like a special offer, unique occasion, or some order deadline that we would like to remind you of.

When you don't hear from us, don't perceive it as a lack of interest or carte blanche to postpone delivery of whatever is scheduled to be done; it's just that we simply are not inclined to maintain close personal contact, and we assume that things are going well, unless informed otherwise.

However, and especially when the business relationship is still young, it can be a good idea to (proactively) send regular updates on the status of a project or delivery. When you receive a request, make sure to reply to it swiftly. When you cannot instantly come up with a satisfying answer, acknowledge receipt and tell the sender by when you will get back to him or her with a response. Expect that your German client would rather write an e-mail; it's up to you to take the opportunity to pick up the phone and build a (more) personal rapport.

Germans like their business partners to be "zuverlässig" (reliable) and things to be predictable. Keep your side of the bargain, and don't make compromises on quality and delivery times. Do not try renegotiating when you have committed to something. If you are buying from

Germans, let them do their job (there is generally no need to constantly follow-up with them either), and if you are not happy with their work, tell them so frankly. Say "yes" when you mean "yes," and "no" when you mean "no."

Develop your relationship(s) step-by-step; be reliable and precise even with the smallest of things, always. Do one thing at a time, and acknowledge that Germans, overall, plan over a comparably long horizon and include more contingencies in plans. Do not challenge Germans by, what they might perceive as, painting castles in the air or suggesting high-risk adventures.

Don't take our bluntness to heart (I apologize for that!), and gently help us understand that sometimes, there is more than just *one* way (read: *our* way). Answer all our "what if" questions to our full satisfaction, highlight your expertise, and finally, win us over by delivering consistently on set objectives; demand the same from us.

I do not subscribe to the idea that, in the business world, you cannot build and maintain cordial relationships with Germans, or even become friends. On the contrary, but it's better not to come *too* close, *too* quickly. And, don't maneuver a German into a situation in which he or she might feel compromised.

Do not expect us to give you special treatment or a "better" price just because we went to a football match together. Don't expect us to bend company regulations and compliance rules just because we stood together on the beer benches and sang binge drinking songs at the Oktoberfest. And, even though we most probably love gifts and surprises as much as everyone else, take care that your present does not exceed the limit allowed by (our) compliance regulations. A German might (in *any* case) tend to perceive a present more valuable than a bottle of standard, good-quality wine as attempted bribery and would refrain from endowing you for the same reasons. So, when we visit you, forgive us for coming with empty hands.

Varied Interpretations of the Term "Hospitality"

Why would I talk about hospitality only at the end of the book when, maybe for you, socializing is essential for trust-building in the *initial* stages of a business relationship? Because, for Germans, "spending time together" typically comes only *after* a deal has been closed. We would (read: might) buy you a meal on having signed a contract. Inviting our top clients for lunch from time to time comes under "Beziehungspflege" (translated word for word as "relationship maintenance" or "relationship cultivation"); rarely would one spend an entire day with a client or supplier, unless invited for a business roadshow or "Tag der offenen Tür" (open house).

When I, for the first time, came across the term "hospitality" (in English), I confused it with the word "hostility." Whoever explained the difference to me must have been an Indian, because it was there that I first heard (of) the term, and ever since, the expression "hospitality" for me is connected with a concept that goes *far beyond* what is commonly understood by the German word "Gastfreundschaft."

In a radio report about "Deutsche Gastfreundschaft," a correspondent from Iran summarized his experience, saying that in Germany, "'beschränkt sich Gastfreundschaft auf ein Glas Wasser aus der Leitung und, wenn es hochkommt, einen Kaffee'" ("hospitality is limited to a glass of water from the tap, and if you are lucky, a cup of coffee") (Wilke 2017). Having once visited a colleague near Nuremberg, he narrates, he had to sleep on an ancient couch. Next to him slept the dog, who at least had a pillow. "'Im Iran hätte ich als Gast das beste Bett bekommen und der Gastgeber hätte auf diesem altersschwachen Sofa gelegen'" ("in Iran, as a guest, I would have had the best bed, and the host would have slept on this age-worn sofa"). Having in mind what is common practice in *his* home country, what he experienced could, by some, indeed be perceived as "hostility."

An interviewee from Hungary, on a scale of 1 to 10, would give us a five on the subject of hospitality, while a Mexican correspondent points out that "Die Deutschen sind aber eher auf den zweiten Blick gastfreundlich. Wenn sie einen einladen und bewirten, dann ist das ganz ernst gemeint. Daraus entstehen richtige Freundschaften, die auch ein Leben halten" ("Germans are usually hospitable (only) at second sight. When they invite and entertain you, they are sincere in their pursuit of a meaningful relationship. The result is real friendships that last a lifetime") (ibid. 2017).

One of my Chinese clients once told me how he, whenever he is in Munich for a bi-annual fair, is invited to one of his clients' homes for dinner. To my ears, that sounded like the ultimate honor, like when you are granted a knighthood. Either they were sourcing *the* most critical components from him, I thought, or they must *really* like this guy.

Germans are rather protective of their private lives and think twice before they invite someone to their homes. When traveling through Morocco a few years ago, and while facing some difficulties in finding accommodation at short notice, I ended up spending one night on the sofa of a young lady I had just met on the bus; even during my student days, it most likely would never have occurred to me to offer a place to stay to someone I didn't know.

When I traveled to Bangalore in 2001, for what I remember was the 45th anniversary of the Indo-German Chamber of Commerce, one of my Indian friends arranged for my accommodation: I slept in the children's room at his cousin's place. The daughter of the house slept with the mother, while the father, whom I only met the next morning, had to move to the living room. When I last visited Delhi, I took the opportunity to also meet a potential business contact, whom I had only been in e-mail contact with before; not only was I invited to his house, he also suggested that I bring along any friends or relatives I would feel (more) comfortable with. He informed me upfront that there would be only vegetarian food and asked about food preferences so that his wife could arrange for my favorite dishes. As he knows Germans, I was offered chilled beer that I could enjoy while I was gently forced to unpack a very generous welcome present. After dinner, the entire family hopped into the car to jointly drive me back to my place. If *you* think "so what?," be prepared for the discovery that Germans are somewhat different.

Not only are we hesitant to give people access to our private homes, we are also not overly generous with gifts, and so on when invited to visit others. I know a lady from France who moved to Germany some 20 years ago; "In my first years ," she told me, "I was single, and I cultivated several friendships to have a social life and exchange with people." She often invited people to dinner at her house. At that time, she did not have much money, while her friends mostly had better jobs, or as couples, had two incomes. "It happened very often that some persons always came with empty hands, something you would never do in France," she complained to me. Recently, she was invited for an informal dinner (bread, cheese, and red wine), and again, she was surprised to see what the other guests brought—one person came empty-handed and another with a very small homemade item, while my friend brought a basket full of food and wine to share. Most probably, *I* would also not have brought more than a bottle of wine, and maybe a gift-wrapped paperback novel. Basically, people had been *invited*, hadn't they?

Osman Bayazit Genc from Istanbul points out that an "Einladung" does "not mean the same as in our culture, so sometimes I have to ask what the invitation covers." That could indeed be a good idea; better ask what exactly is planned, and what you can/are supposed to bring. The "average" German would appreciate you inquiring.

When you invite us, assume that we will show up "pünktlich" (if not up to 10 minutes early). Andreas Hauser told me how, in Brazil, some Germans arrived at a party at the mentioned starting time, only there was no party because the hosts were still out grocery shopping!

Lukas Schmitz, a German who works in Mumbai, shared the following episode with me: Last year, he flew to Germany to spend Christmas with his family. On the final leg of the journey, when flying from Munich to Hamburg, he sat next to an Indian who had been living and working in Germany for two years. They started to talk, and the Indian gentleman casually said that he found it a pity that he had to be in Germany now. Schmitz was surprised and asked: "Why is that? Christmas is the best time of the year; everything is white and Christmassy-decorated." His seat neighbor agreed, but explained that, because Germans celebrate Christmas only with the closest family circle and rarely even invite friends to celebrate with them, *he* was about to spend the next three or four days at home, alone in his apartment, with no idea how to keep himself busy. Schmitz found this statement very interesting and true, reflecting great cultural differences, especially when you compare Germany with India. "When I think about how, in India, Diwali is celebrated," he wrote, "and nobody needs to be alone because everyone is invited to many festivities, I could understand my seat neighbor's sad vibes; it was an unfortunate thing because, for us, Christmas is actually the feast of love."

What's my point? Firstly, please don't feel disappointed, upset, or even offended if you, when traveling to Germany, are not welcomed as warmly as you would assume is polite or decent, by your own standards. When a German suggests that you visit a restaurant together in the evening (after *Feierabend*), that is generally a *very* good sign.

Secondly, if you are hosting Germans, take care not to tax them with your (understanding of) hospitality. For example, try to give them some space; do not feel that you must entertain them from early morning until late evening. We are generally not used to that much attention and interaction, and it can make us feel uneasy. You may offer us a place to sleep at your house, but don't be surprised if we would rather stay at a hotel. When taking care of lodging, assume that your guest will prefer a quiet place over a hotel that is located in the most happening part of town. When making a reservation, insist on a non-smoker room (unless explicitly requested otherwise), and in case you prepare a bed for the night in your house, turn down the air conditioning a bit—a German might easily freeze at what you consider a "pleasant" temperature (the same applies to meeting rooms).

When spending more than just one afternoon together, from time to time, I suggest you ask your visitors whether they would like to take some rest (read: enjoy some privacy). Don't chauffeur your visitor through the country for hours; no matter how much we might love cars, we tend to have a much lower tolerance level for prolonged sitting. Always tell your guests what's next; instead of "we'll pick you up after lunch," better tell them "we'll give you a call from the reception at around three in the afternoon."

Help them understand how you like to spend your evenings when you invite them home for dinner. One of my Indian aunties (may God rest her soul), for example, told me, "In India, first we drink, then we eat, and then we fall into our beds." That was the most valuable intel for me. Tell your guest, so Frau Vogt doesn't have to fear that there will be no food, and before Dr. Sittel concludes he has joined a group of alcoholics. In Germany, the "hard stuff" like whisky is served only *after* dinner, and then, it may turn out that the visitors sit there forever. Tell Frau Krumm if, in contrast, the dinner guests would usually leave quite abruptly; otherwise, she might think that something has just gone terribly wrong!

Don't attempt persistently talking your guest into tasting this and that, or having one more helping. Usually, a German would finish his or her plate, and if still hungry, would ask for, or rather, not decline another helping. No need to insist! If we would like to have some tea, we would generally simply say "yes, please" if offered some, or reply "only if it's no inconvenience to you."

You will most likely sense when your guest is somewhat familiar with your culture's habits; if your visitor has memorized some dos and don'ts (of how to "normally" behave in your country), it may otherwise become tricky if you *strictly* follow my advice. However, no matter how much the person knows about the etiquette in your country, please don't "force" your guest to, for instance, taste chicken feet, bull penis, or dried squid. Some foods simply don't appeal to our taste buds or are taboo for other reasons, and while you might feel sad or offended when we decline, your guest might feel like throwing up when only *thinking* about the offer.

Germans tend to consume less sugar than people in many other places, so don't be surprised if the dessert remains untouched. Generally, it is always a good idea to (also) offer something light and vegetarian; not too much fast food, if possible. Unpack the food (like chutneys or sandwiches) before serving it and choose china plates over plastic dishes. Irrespective of the jetlag your guest may experience, consider that a German might feel hungry before your "normal" mealtimes. We are not used to eating after 8 o'clock in the evening, for instance.

It is certainly up to you if you want to ditch someone over declining your dinner invitation, because, for example, he or she would argue that, unfortunately, he or she has already checked in for the return flight to Düsseldorf. However, keep in mind that your potential business partner typically would have flown to Moscow only to "talk shop," planning only the time needed to travel to your office and back. Herr Lamprecht might not have a clue that he is not only missing a very good opportunity, but also offending you. And, think twice before jumping to (the wrong) conclusion when Frau Memminger declines your very generous surprise gift.

Speaking of presents, there are some items you should (also) be careful with. Some years ago, an Indian gentleman gifted me red roses as a welcome present, when he came to pick me up from my hotel room (don't do that either!) in Chandigarh. I felt very confused and uncomfortable because, in Germany, only someone in love with you would gift you that particular flower. You can bring flowers when invited to a dinner party in Germany, but better tell the florist what the purpose of the gift is and who the recipient is; there are flowers for love, for funerals, and so on. Also, it would be better not to present a bouquet with (the unlucky number of) 13 flowers. Typically, a bottle of wine, chocolates, or a fruit basket are good options. If you bring something from your country, that will also be appreciated. Some small decorative item, like a pen holder for the office or a wall calendar, for example, is also an appropriate gift. Consider the gift wrapping carefully; I am not talking only about *how* you wrap the paper (Germans are rather negligent in this department), but about the paper itself. It is better to choose a rather simple, not too glittery, paper, for ecological reasons and considering taste preferences. Take care that the paper does not smell intensely of print color or carry traces of naphthalene. Don't gift us something with a Swastika on it because, for us, the symbol relates to the (unpleasant memory of the) Nazi Hakenkreuz.

Compliment your hosts for their good taste in furniture and home decor, show interest in the books that are displayed on the shelf (but "please don't touch!"), and tell them how much you like the food; but be careful with complimenting the lady of the house for anything that (for you) might be typically "women's business." It is advisable to generally be careful with paying compliments to German women, especially during business meetings: Pointing out that it is a pleasure to talk to such an attractive lady will easily give the woman you are addressing the idea that you are unprofessional, immature, afraid of women, or just stupid. Once, a potential client told me over dinner, when I put down my specs to enjoy my steaming soup, "Without glasses, you are beautiful!" Even if you are utterly surprised by the previously hidden beauty of your prospective business partner, just swallow it. Yes, some flirting, if appropriate, might not harm, even in a business situation, but don't forget if you are talking to a person from another background/culture, chances are high that he or she is not familiar with "your" savoir-faire. But, it is still a good idea to hold the door for women (and men, too!) or help the other person with her (or his) coat—you wouldn't see that very often, but if some gentleman struggles, you can help.

When you are having lunch or dinner is a better time to exchange more non-business-related thoughts than during the "typical German" two-minute-or-so small talk. Germans like to hear compliments about "Made in Germany," but at the same time, as individuals, often prefer being considered "not a typical German" (that is regarded as a compliment). Your knowledge of German history will surely be appreciated, but pointing out how Hitler must be admired for his leadership skills is really not a smart move, trust me! If you want to flatter your companion, better talk about Germany as a great football nation or the beautiful places you have visited/heard of.

Germans like to have a "meaningful conversation," although German resident Neil Deane from Liverpool writes in his book, *Modern Germany*, that "the German might regard what we call an argument ... as a meaningful discussion" (Deane 2014). Please don't feel offended when people tell you how much they condemn any deficiencies observed in your homeland, which one can easily point a finger at from afar. Poverty, child labor, pollution, narrow-minded political leaders, one-child policy ... you name it. Or—heaven forbid!—arranged marriage. I am not saying that you should not contradict or contribute your perspective, but sometimes, in my humble opinion, it's better to just try to change the subject. Ask what their plans are for the next holiday, or inquire whether the Sunday evening crime-serial *Tatort* is worth watching.

The aforementioned are normally "safe" questions; people would not feel offended or awkward to respond. Never ask a woman why she's not married (heaven forbid!), or why people don't have children. Depending on where you come from, asking questions about one's marital status, existence of children, digestion, or salary might be part of getting to know another person; most Germans would perceive these questions as far too personal.

You may show a photo or two of your family, but leave it at that. No need to show a picture of your daughter at her graduation, on her last birthday, the one before that, at the Diwali party, Christmas party, on holiday in Goa, holiday in Thailand ... *yawn!*

When invited to a German home, it might be a bit tricky for you to figure out when your hosts expect you to leave; I suggest that, after dessert and coffee, which is maybe served along with a digestif (cognac or schnapps, which you don't need to accept), you inquire about until when a taxi (or train or bus) will be available, so you can be told what would be the best option to choose (including timing).

I think now, it's time for me to call it a day, too. At this point, I have nothing more to add, except for wishing you well with your future (business) encounters with Germans.

All the best!

Feierabend

References

Abelshauser, W. 2012. “Ricardo neu gedacht: Komparative institutionelle Vorteile von Wirtschaftskulturen.” In *Kulturen der Weltwirtschaft*, eds. W. Abelshauser, D.A. Gilgen and A. Leutzsch. Göttingen: Vandenhoeck & Ruprecht.

Abelshauser, W. September, 2018. “Wunder gibt es immer wieder: Mythos Wirtschaftswunder.” *Aus Politik und Zeitgeschichte*, pp. 4–10.

Absolventa GmbH. 2018. “Durchschnittsgehalt in Deutschland” [Average salary in Germany]. *absolventa.de*. https://absolventa.de/karriereguide/arbeitsentgelt/durchschnittsgehalt (accessed July 29, 2018).

ADAC e.V. 2018. “Fragen und Antworten zu Fahrverboten in Deutschland.” *adac.de*. https://adac.de/rund-ums-fahrzeug/abgas-diesel-fahrverbote/fahrverbote/dieselfahrverbot-faq/ (accessed October 24, 2018).

Albrecht, F. 2018. “SPD-Mitgliederentscheid: So stimmt die SPD über die große Koalition ab.” *zeit.de*. https://zeit.de/politik/deutschland/2018-02/spd-mitgliederentscheid-grosse-koalition-faq (accessed August 5, 2018).

Alpha History. n.d. “The Great Depression in Germany.” *alphahistory.com*. https://alphahistory.com/weimarrepublic/great-depression/ (accessed July 8, 2018).

ARD-aktuell / tagesschau.de. 2017. “Bundestagswahl 2017: Deutschland.” *https://wahl.tagesschau.de*. https://wahl.tagesschau.de/wahlen/2017-09-24-BT-DE/index.shtml (accessed October 24, 2018).

AUMA—Association of the German Trade Fair Industry. n.d. “Find Your Trade Fair.” *auma.de*. https://auma.de/en/exhibit/find-your-exhibitions (accessed October 19, 2018).

AUMA—Austellungs- und Messe-Ausschuss der Deutschen Wirtschaft e.V., ed. 2015. *AUMA_MesseGuide Deutschland 2016*. Berlin: n.p.

Bax, M. n.d. “Das Schulsystem in Deutschland – Funktionen und Aufgaben.” *bildungsxperten.net*. https://bildungsxperten.net/wissen/das-schulsystem-in-deutschland-funktionen-und-aufgaben/ (accessed October 21, 2018).

Bleiker, C. 2017. “A Minority Government in Germany: What You Need to Know.” *dw.com*. https://dw.com/en/a-minority-government-in-germany-what-you-need-to-know/a-41618320 (accessed August 4, 2018).

Bolz, F. 2014. “Wozu überhaupt Latein und Altgriechisch lernen?” *welt.de*. https://welt.de/politik/deutschland/article126437070/Wozu-ueberhaupt-Latein-und-Altgriechisch-lernen.html (accessed October 23, 2018).

Borchmeyer, D. 2017. *Was ist deutsch?: Die Suche einer Nation nach sich selbst*. Berlin: Rowohlt Berlin Verlag.

Braun, K., and F. Diekmann. 2017. "So arbeitet Deutschland: Auf dem Weg in die Teilzeitrepublik." *spiegel.de*. http://spiegel.de/wirtschaft/soziales/arbeitszeit-so-arbeitet-deutschland-auf-einen-blick-a-1158784.html (accessed September 22, 2018).

Buchan, N. 2009. "The Complexity of Trust: Cultural Environments, Trust, and Trust Development." In *Cambridge Handbook of Culture, Organizations, and Work*, eds. R.S. Bhagat and R.M. Steers. Cambridge: Cambridge University Press.

Bundesagentur für Arbeit. 2018a. "Beschäftigte." *statistik.arbeitsagentur.de*. https://statistik.arbeitsagentur.de/Navigation/Statistik/Statistik-nach-Themen/Beschaeftigung/Beschaeftigung-Nav.html (accessed June 13, 2018).

Bundesagentur für Arbeit. 2018b. "Entgeltatlas 2017." *entgeltatlas.arbeitsagentur.de*. https://entgeltatlas.arbeitsagentur.de/entgeltatlas (accessed October 19, 2018).

Bundesministerium der Finanzen. 2018. "Steuern von A bis Z: Ausgabe 2018." *bundesfinanzministerium.de*. https://bundesfinanzministerium.de/Content/DE/Downloads/Broschueren_Bestellservice/2018-03-26-steuern-von-a-z.pdf?__blob=publicationFile&v=18 (accessed October 23, 2018).

Bundesministerium für Bildung und Forschung. n.d. "Dekade für Alphabetisierung." *www.bmbf.de*. https://bmbf.de/de/nationale-strategie-fuer-alphabetisierung-und-grundbildung-erwachsener-1373.html (accessed October 21, 2018).

Bundesministerium für Wirtschaft und Energie. 2018a. "Dienstleistungen sichtbar gemacht: Zahlen und Trends auf einen Blick" [Making services visible: figures and trends at a glance]. *bmwi.de*. https://bmwi.de/Redaktion/DE/Artikel/Mittelstand/dienstleistungswirtschaft-01-zahlen-trends.html (accessed September 22, 2018).

Bundesministerium für Wirtschaft und Energie. 2018b. "Gewerbe, die zu Anlage A zählen (Handwerksberufe mit Meisterpflicht)." *BMWi Behördenwegweiser*. http://bmwi-wegweiser.de/download/handwerk_a_berufe.pdf (accessed October 21, 2018).

Bundesverband der Deutschen Industrie e.V. (BDI). n.d. "BDI: Members." *english.bdi.eu*. https://english.bdi.eu/bdi/members/ (accessed October 23, 2018).

Bundeszentrale für politische Bildung. 2018. "Ausgewählte Armutsgefährdungsquoten." *bpb.de*. http://bpb.de/nachschlagen/zahlen-und-fakten/soziale-situation-in-deutschland/61785/armutsgefaehrdung (accessed October 23, 2018).

Cremer, G. 2016. *Armut in Deutschland : Wer ist arm? Was läuft schief? Wie können wir handeln?* Bonn: Bundeszentrale für Politische Bildung.

Czollek, M. 2018. *Desintegriert Euch!* München: Hanser.

Czycholl, H. 2014. "Die 'German Angst' steckt tief in unseren Genen" [The "German fear" is deep in our genes]. *welt.de*. https://welt.de/wissenschaft/article132728527/Die-German-Angst-steckt-tief-in-unseren-Genen.html (accessed September 26, 2018).

Das Leben der Anderen. 2006. Directed by Florian Henckel von Donnersmarck.

Day, M. 2013. "Nazis May have Killed up to 20m, Claims 'Shocking' New Holocaust Study." *telegraph.co.uk*. https://telegraph.co.uk/news/worldnews/europe/germany/9906771/Nazis-may-have-killed-up-to-20m-claims-shocking-new-Holocaust-study.html (accessed July 9, 2018).

Deane, N. 2014. *Modern Germany: An Outsider's View from the Inside*. Berlin: Pro BUSINESS.

Deutsche Handwerks Zeitung. 2016. "Meister werden: Was Sie wissen müssen." *deutsche-handwerks-zeitung.de*. https://deutsche-handwerks-zeitung.de/der-weg-zum-meister-was-sie-wissen-muessen/150/3096/202711 (accessed October 21, 2018).

Deutsche Nationalbibliothek. n.d. "Letters of Indulgence : Early Printed Materials and Objects of Dispute During the Reformation." *mediengeschichte.dnb.de*. http://mediengeschichte.dnb.de/DBSMZBN/Content/EN/Printing/04-ablassbriefe-en.html (accessed July 5, 2018).

Deutsche Welle. 2012. "125 years of 'Made in Germany.'" *dw.com*. https://dw.com/en/125-years-of-made-in-germany/a-16188583 (accessed June 13, 2018).

Deutsche Welle. 2018. "Mindestlohn in Deutschland soll steigen." *dw.com*. https://dw.com/de/mindestlohn-in-deutschland-soll-steigen/a-44401699 (accessed October 23, 2018).

Deutscher Industrie- und Handelskammertag (DIHK) e.V. n.d. *www.ahk.de/en/*. https://ahk.de/en/locations/ahk-locations/ (accessed November 6, 2018).

Die Armutsindustrie. 2009. Produced by Eva Müller.

Die Deutsche Wirtschaft. 2016. "The Best in Germany: the 10,000 Most Important Medium-Sized Companies." *die-deutsche-wirtschaft.de*. https://die-deutsche-wirtschaft.de/the-best-in-germany-the-10000-most-important-medium-sized-companies/ (accessed June 19, 2018).

Die Deutsche Wirtschaft. 2018. "Ranking der Bundesländer nach Top-Mittelständlern." *die-deutsche-wirtschaft.de*. https://die-deutsche-wirtschaft.de/ranking-der-bundeslaender-nach-top-mittelstaendlern/ (accessed October 18, 2018).

DIN Deutsches Institut für Normung e.V. n.d. *https://din.de/en* (accessed October 22, 2018).

Djahangard, S. 2018. "Solidaritätszuschlag: Behalten oder nicht." *zeit.de*. https://zeit.de/2018/37/solidaritaetszuschlag-abschaffen-bundesregierung (accessed October 24, 2018).

DLG Service GmbH. n.d. "Facts & Figures : Review of AGRITECHNICA 2017." *agritechnica.com.* https://agritechnica.com/en/for-exhibitors/facts-figures/ (accessed October 19, 2018).

Drobinski, M., and J. Wetzel. 2018. "Kreuz-Erlass : Kardinal Marx wirft Söder Spaltung vor." *sueddeutsche.de.* https://sueddeutsche.de/bayern/kreuz-erlass-kardinal-marx-wirft-soeder-spaltung-vor-1.3962223 (accessed October 18, 2018).

Dumont, R. 2013. *Paradiessucher* [Paradise Seekers]. München: Hanser Verlag.

Ebert, F., B. Kruse, M. Schories, and M. Zajonz. n.d. "So sehr belastet die Miete die Münchner." *projekte.sueddeutsche.de.* https://projekte.sueddeutsche.de/artikel/muenchen/meinemiete-so-stark-belastet-die-miete-die-muenchner-e807307/ (accessed October 23, 2018).

Eddy, M. 2017. "After Tumultuous Week, Germany's Politics Look to the Familiar." *nytimes.com.* https://nytimes.com/2017/11/27/world/europe/germany-merkel-government.html (accessed August 5, 2018).

Europäische Kommission. 2018. "Eurostat Pressemitteilung: Abwärtstrend beim Anteil der von Armut oder sozialer Ausgrenzung bedrohten Personen in der EU." *ec.europa.eu/eurostat.* https://ec.europa.eu/eurostat/documents/2995521/9310038/3-16102018-BP-DE.pdf/dafea596-6e56-4971-a7c3-f096fb6f6cb5 (accessed October 23, 2018).

European Central Bank. n.d. "Use of the Euro." *ecb.europa.eu.* https://ecb.europa.eu/euro/intro/html/index.en.html (accessed July 27, 2018).

Federal Ministry for Economic Affairs and Energy. n.d. "German States at a Glance." *make-it-in-germany.com.* https://make-it-in-germany.com/en/for-qualified-professionals/discover-germany/german-states-at-a-glance (accessed September 18, 2018).

Federal Statistical Office. n.d. *Statistisches Bundesamt (Destatis), 2018.* https://destatis.de/EN/Homepage.html

Fletcher, A. 2015. *How to be German: In 50 Easy Steps. A Guide from Apfelsaftschorle to Tschüss.* München: Verlag C.H. Beck oHG.

Forschungsgruppe Weltanschauungen in Deutschland und der Welt (fowid). 2017. "Religionszugehörigkeiten in Deutschland 2016." *fowid.de.* https://fowid.de/meldung/religionszugehoerigkeiten-deutschland-2016 (accessed June 9, 2018).

Frankfurter Buchmesse GmbH. 2018. "70. Frankfurter Buchmesse: internationale Beteiligung wächst / dynamisches Lizenzgeschäft / Menschenrechte im Fokus / BOOKFEST begeistert das Publikum." *buchmesse.de.* https://buchmesse.de/presse/pressemitteilungen/2018-10-14-70-frankfurter-buchmesse (accessed October 19, 2018).

Frankfurter Neue Presse. 2018. "Frankfurt wächst bis Herbst auf 750.000 Einwohner." *fnp.de.* http://fnp.de/lokales/frankfurt/Frankfurt-waechst-bis-Herbst-auf-750-000-Einwohner;art675,2970702 (accessed October 17, 2018).

Frerk, C. 2017. "Bedeutung von Religion in Deutschland 2017, 2015, 2012, 2011, 2008." *fowid.de.* https://fowid.de/meldung/bedeutung-religion-deutschland-2017-2015-2012-2011-2008 (accessed June 9, 2018).

Fulbrook, M. 2004. *A Concise History of Germany.* Cambridge: Cambridge University Press.

Good Bye, Lenin! 2003. Directed by Wolfgang Becker.

Hernandez, R.A. 2013. *Presenting Across Cultures: How to Adapt Your Business and Sales Presentations in Key Markets Around the World.* Norderstedt: BoD.

Hofstede, G., G.J. Hofstede, and M. Minkov. 2010. *Cultures and Organizations - Software of the Mind: Intercultural Cooperation and Its Importance for Survival.* New York, NY: McGraw-Hill.

Höhne, G. 2014. "Virtuelle Teams zusammenschweißen." *Personalwirtschaft,* pp. 58–59.

Holzbach-Linsenmaier, H. 1994. "Dem Führer ein Kind schenken." *zeit.de.* https://zeit.de/1994/19/dem-fuehrer-ein-kind-schenken/seite-3 (accessed October 25, 2018).

Huggler, J. 2017. "'We are an Open Society. We Show Our Face. We are Not Burka,' Says German Interior Minister." *telegraph.co.uk.* https://telegraph.co.uk/news/2017/04/30/open-society-show-face-not-burka-says-german-interior-minister/ (accessed October 18, 2018).

Immowelt AG. 2018. "Mietspiegel in Görlitz." *immowelt.de.* https://immowelt.de/immobilienpreise/landkreis-goerlitz/mietspiegel (accessed October 23, 2018).

Institut für Mittelstandsforschung Bonn. n.d. "KMU-Definition des IfM Bonn." *ifm-bonn.org.* https://ifm-bonn.org/definitionen/kmu-definition-des-ifm-bonn/ (accessed October 18, 2018).

Interbrand. n.d. "Best Global Brands 2017." *interbrand.com.* https://interbrand.com/best-brands/best-global-brands/2017/ranking/ (accessed June 19, 2018).

Jobware GmbH. 2018. "Brutto Netto Rechner – Gehaltsrechner für 2018." *jobware.de.* https://jobware.de/Gehaltsrechner (accessed October 19, 2018).

Knapp, P., ed. 2017. *Verhandlungs-Tools: Effiziente Verhandlungstechniken im Business-Alltag.* Bonn: managerSeminare Verlags GmbH.

Kraftfahrt-Bundesamt. n.d. "Kraftfahrt-Bundesamt – Verkehrsauffälligkeiten." *kba.de.* https://kba.de/DE/Statistik/Kraftfahrer/Verkehrsauffaelligkeiten/verkehrsauffaelligkeiten_node.html#rechts (accessed June 2, 2018).

Kreuter, D. 2014. *Erfolgreich akquirieren auf Messen.* Wiesbaden: Springer Fachmedien.

Kühne, S., O. Schnuck, and R. Schöffel. 2017. "Der Computer sagt: Jamaika." *web.br.de.* https://web.br.de/interaktiv/wahlprogramm-analyse-bundestagswahl/ (accessed August 6, 2018).

Landeszentrale für politische Bildung Baden-Württemberg. n.d. "Bundestagswahl 2013." *bundestagswahl-bw.de.* http://bundestagswahl-bw.de/wahlergebnis_btwahl2013.html (accessed August 5, 2018).

MacGregor, N. 2016. *Germany: Memories of a Nation*. London: Penguin Books.

Magee, J.O. 2018a. "Business Mentality: Germans Consult, Americans Serve." *global.handelsblatt.com*. https://global.handelsblatt.com/opinion/germans-consult-americans-serve-942418 (accessed October 4, 2018).

Magee, J.O. 2018b. "Lost in Translation : German Directness, American Euphemisms: The Hell of Cross-Cultural Communication." *global.handelsblatt.com*. https://global.handelsblatt.com/opinion/german-directness-american-euphemisms-hell-cross-cultural-communication-891303 (accessed October 4, 2018).

MAPfrappe–Compare Geo Sizes, Copyright © 2018 by Kelvin Thompson. All Rights Reserved. 2018. *mapfrappe.com* (accessed June 9, 2018).

Messe München GmbH. n.d. "Fakten zur bauma: Alles über die Weltleitmesse." *bauma.de*. https://bauma.de/messe/informieren/daten-fakten/ (accessed October 19, 2018).

Meyer, E. 2015. *The Culture Map: Decoding How People Think, Lead, and Get Things Done Across Cultures*. New York, NY: PublicAffairs.

Mokyr, J. 1998. "The Second Industrial Revolution, 1870–1914." *semanticscholar.org*. https://pdfs.semanticscholar.org/769c/a06c2ea1ab122e0e2a37099be00e3c11dd52.pdf (accessed July 20, 2018).

Münkler, H. 2010. *Die Deutschen und ihre Mythen* [The Germans and their myths]. Reinbeck bei Hamburg: Rowohlt Taschenbuch Verlag.

Muschter, G., and R. Thomas. 2015. *Frauen in Deutschland – Eine Geschichte in Bildern, Quellen und Kommentaren*. Bonn: Bundeszentrale für politische Bildung.

Preker, A. 2017. "Studie zur Rente : Altersarmut nimmt in Deutschland drastisch zu." *spiegel.de*. http://spiegel.de/wirtschaft/soziales/altersarmut-nimmt-in-deutschland-drastisch-zu-a-1153561.html (accessed September 22, 2018).

Presse- und Informationsamt der Bundesregierung. 2018. "JAHRESWIRTSCHAFTSBERICHT 2018: Wirtschaft weiter in guter Verfassung." *bundesregierung.de*. https://bundesregierung.de/Content/DE/Artikel/2018/01/2018-01-31-jahreswirtschaftsbericht-2018.html (accessed September 22, 2018).

Riemhofer, A. 2014. *Interkulturelle Kinder- und Jugendliteratur in Deutschland: Lesen auf eigene Gefahr*. Marburg: Tectum Wissenschaftsverlag.

Riemhofer, A. 2017. *The What, Why and How of Attending Trade Shows in Germany: Hands-on Advice for both Visitors and Exhibitors*. e-Book. München: ANDRA.

Rundfunk Berlin-Brandenburg (rbb). 2018. "Neue Einwohnerzahlen : Mehr als 3,7 Millionen Menschen leben in Berlin." *rbb24.de*. https://rbb24.de/panorama/beitrag/2018/10/berlin-einwohner-bevoelkerung-zuwachs.html (accessed October 17, 2018).

Schaefer, L. 2008. "68 Movement Brought Lasting Changes to German Society." *dw.com*. https://dw.com/en/68-movement-brought-lasting-changes-to-german-society/a-3257581 (accessed July 9, 2018).

Schroll-Machl, S. 2008. *Doing Business with Germans: Their Perception, Our Perception*. Göttingen: Vandenhoeck & Ruprecht.

Schubert, K. 2018. "Arbeitsentgelte im Vergleich – Wie es an Ihrem Arbeitsort aussieht." *zdf.de*. https://zdf.de/nachrichten/heute/so-unterschiedlich-verdienen-die-deutschen-100.html (accessed October 23, 2018).

Schugk, M. 2004. *Interkulturelle Werbung: Kulturbedingte Unterschiede in Verkauf und Werbung*. München: Verlag Franz Vahlen GmbH.

Schulenburg, N. 2018. *Exzellent präsentieren: Die Psychologie erfolgreicher Ideenvermittlung – Werkzeuge und Techniken für herausragende Präsentationen*. Wiesbaden: Springer Gabler.

Schymura, Y. 2014. "Frauen im Nationalsozialismus: 'Das Mutterkreuz ist mein sehnlichster Wunsch.'" *spiegel.de*. http://spiegel.de/einestages/mutterkreuze-unter-hitler-mutterkult-im-nationalsozialismus-a-967822.html (accessed October 25, 2018).

Şenocak, Z. 2011. *Deutschsein : Eine Aufklärungsschrift*. Hamburg: edition Körber-Stiftung.

Simon, H. 2012. *Hidden Champions – Aufbruch nach Globalia: die Erfolgsstrategien unbekannter Weltmarktführer*. Frankfurt am Main: Campus-Verlag.

Staatsministerium Baden-Württemberg. n.d. "The State and Its People." *baden-wuerttemberg.de*. https://baden-wuerttemberg.de/en/our-state/the-state-and-its-people/ (accessed June 20, 2019).

Statista GmbH. 2018a. "Entwicklung der Gesamtzahl der anerkannten oder als anerkannt geltenden Ausbildungsberufe in Deutschland von 1971 bis 2017." *de.statista.com*. https://de.statista.com/statistik/daten/studie/156901/umfrage/ausbildungsberufe-in-deutschland/ (accessed October 19, 2018).

Statista GmbH. 2018b. "Statistiken zum Thema Familie." *de.statista.com*. https://de.statista.com/themen/98/familie/ (accessed June 9, 2018).

Statistisches Bundesamt. 2015. "Risk of poverty in Germany at 16.7%." *destatis.de*. https://destatis.de/EN/FactsFigures/SocietyState/IncomeConsumptionLivingConditions/LivingConditionsRiskPoverty/Current_KeyIndicators_SILC.html (accessed October 23, 2018).

Statistisches Bundesamt. 2017: "19.7% of Germany's Population at Risk of Poverty or Social Exclusion." *destatis.de*. https://destatis.de/EN/PressServices/Press/pr/2017/11/PE17_392_634.html (accessed July 29, 2018).

Statistisches Bundesamt. 2018a. "Arbeitsmarkt."*destatis.de*. https://destatis.de/DE/ZahlenFakten/Indikatoren/LangeReihen/Arbeitsmarkt/lrerw013.html (accessed September 22, 2018).

Statistisches Bundesamt. 2018b. "Bundesländer mit Hauptstädten nach Fläche, Bevölkerung und Bevölkerungsdichte am 31.12.2016." *destatis.de*. https://destatis.de/DE/ZahlenFakten/LaenderRegionen/Regionales/Gemeindeverzeichnis/Administrativ/Aktuell/02Bundeslaender.html (accessed October 22, 2018).

Statistisches Bundesamt. 2018c. "Consumption expenditure – Germany." *destatis.de*. https://destatis.de/EN/FactsFigures/SocietyState/IncomeConsumptionLivingConditions/ConsumptionExpenditure/Tables/PrivateConsumption_D.html (accessed July 29, 2018).

Statistisches Bundesamt. 2018d. "Haushalte & Familien." *destatis.de*. https://destatis.de/DE/ZahlenFakten/GesellschaftStaat/Bevoelkerung/HaushalteFamilien/HaushalteFamilien.html (accessed August 18, 2018).

Statistisches Bundesamt. 2018e. "Konsumausgaben privater Haushalte: Nahrungsmittel." *destatis.de*. https://destatis.de/DE/ZahlenFakten/LaenderRegionen/Internationales/Thema/Tabellen/Basistabelle_KonsumN.html (accessed October 23, 2018).

Statistisches Bundesamt. 2018f. "The Main German Export Product: Motor Vehicles." *destatis.de*. https://destatis.de/EN/FactsFigures/NationalEconomyEnvironment/ForeignTrade/TradingGoods.html (accessed October 24, 2018).

Statistisches Bundesamt. 2018g. "Foreign Trade : Exports and Imports (Special Trade) by Division of the National Product Classification for Production Statistics 2017 (Preliminary Results)." *destatis.de*. https://destatis.de/EN/FactsFigures/NationalEconomyEnvironment/ForeignTrade/Tables/ImportsExports.html (accessed August 5, 2018).

Statistisches Bundesamt. n.d. "Einkommen, Einnahmen & Ausgaben: Einkommen, Einnahmen und Ausgaben privater Haushalte 2016 in den Gebietsständen." *destatis.de*. https://destatis.de/DE/ZahlenFakten/GesellschaftStaat/EinkommenKonsumLebensbedingungen/EinkommenEinnahmenAusgaben/Tabellen/Gebietsstaende.html (accessed October 23, 2018).

Stiftung Internationaler Karlspreis zu Aachen. 2018. "Charlemagne Prize 2018." *karlspreis.de*. https://karlspreis.de/en/news/charlemagne-prize-2018 (accessed July 6, 2018).

Taylor, H. 2018. "Gamescom Sets Another Record for Attendance." *gamesindustry.biz*. https://gamesindustry.biz/articles/2018-08-29-gamescom-sets-another-record-for-attendance (accessed October 19, 2018).

The Foreign Office, London. 2014. *Leitfaden für britische Soldaten in Deutschland 1944 / Instructions for British Servicemen in Germany 1944.* Translated by Klaus Modick. Köln: Kiepenheuer & Witsch.

Thüringer Tourismus GmbH. n.d. "Luther-Worte, die wir vermisst hätten." *lutherland-thueringen.de*. http://lutherland-thueringen.de/de/luther-worte.html (accessed October 25, 2018).

TRADING ECONOMICS. n.d. "Germany GDP per Capita PPP." *trading economics.com.* https://tradingeconomics.com/germany/gdp-per-capita-ppp (accessed July 29, 2018).

Traveler's Digest. 2014. "How Big is Germany in Comparison to the United States, United Kingdom and Japan?" *travelersdigest.com.* http://travelersdigest.com/7356-how-big-is-germany-in-comparison-to-the-united-states-united-kingdom-japan/ (accessed June 9, 2018).

Treber, L. 2014. *Mythos Trümmerfrauen: Von der Trümmerbeseitigung in der Kriegs- und Nachkriegszeit und der Entstehung eines deutschen Erinnerungsortes.* Essen: Klartext Verlag.

Trompenaars, F., and C. Hampden-Turner. 2012. *Riding the Waves of Culture: Understanding Diversity in Global Business.* London and Boston: Nicholas Brealey International.

United States Holocaust Memorial Museum. n.d. "Introduction to the Holocaust." *www.ushmm.org.* https://ushmm.org/wlc/en/article.php?ModuleId=10005143 (accessed July 9, 2018).

VDI Verein Deutscher Ingenieure e.V. n.d. *vdi.de.* https://vdi.de/ueber-uns/vdi-vor-ort/freundeskreise-im-ausland/ (accessed November 6, 2018).

VDMA e.V. – Mechanical Engineering Industry Association. n.d. "VDMA–More than 125 Years with a Finger on the Pulse." *vdma.org.* https://vdma.org/en/ueber-uns#15 (accessed October 21, 2018).

Verband der Automobilindustrie e.V. (VDA). 2017. "IAA Showcases Entire Range of Innovations for Mobility." *vda.de.* https://vda.de/en/press/press-releases/24092017-iaa-showcases-entire-range-of-innovations-for-mobility.html (accessed October 19, 2018).

Verband der Automobilindustrie e.V. (VDA). 2018. "VDA 2018 : Mitglieder." *vda.de.* https://vda.de/de/verband/mitglieder.html (accessed October 20, 2018).

von Goethe, J.W. 2007. *FAUST (First Part): German-English Edition. Translated and with an Introduction and Notes by Peter Salm.* Translated by Peter Salm. New York, NY: Bantam Dell.

Watson, P. 2010. *The German Genius : Europe's Third Renaissance, the Second Scientific Revolution, and the Twentieth Century.* London: Simon & Schuster.

Westdeutscher Rundfunk Köln. 2018. *Ein Jahr nach der Wahl: Verstehen die Bürger diese Regierung noch?* [One year after the election: Do the citizens still understand this government?].

Wilke, E. 2017. "'Typisch deutsch?': Gastfreundschaft." ["Typically German?": Hospitality]. *deutschlandfunkkultur.de.* https://deutschlandfunkkultur.de/typisch-deutsch-gastfreundschaft-die-deutschen-sind-sehr.2857.de.html?dram:article_id=388244 (accessed October 10, 2018).

Wippermann, P., and J. Krüger. 2017. *Werte-Index 2018.* Frankfurt am Main: Deutscher Fachverlag GmbH.

ZEIT ONLINE. 2018. "Bayern schreibt Kreuze in allen Staatsbehörden vor." [Bavaria stipulates that there must be crosses in all state authorities.] *zeit.de*. https://zeit.de/gesellschaft/zeitgeschehen/2018-04/markus-soeder-csu-kreuz-christentum-behoerden-bayern (accessed October 18, 2018).

Zentralverband Elektrotechnik- und Elektronikindustrie e.V. n.d. *zvei.org/en/*. https://zvei.org/en/subjects/markets-law/ (accessed November 6, 2018).

Index

About the Author

Andra Riemhofer is a German native and holds an applied science university diploma in Business Administration, along with an MA in Intercultural Communications and Cooperation. She has more than 20 years of work experience, and her books and other publications on German culture and India have been very well received.

Working as a consultant, she helps international companies enter the German market and avoid the common pitfalls that typically arise from intercultural misunderstandings.

Along with her hands-on intercultural support, she offers research, appointment-setting, handholding, and other sales-related services. Most of her clients are from the UAE, India, and Nordic countries. For further information on her portfolio and business philosophy, please log on to www.andra-ibf.com

OTHER TITLES IN THE INTERNATIONAL BUSINESS COLLECTION

Tamer Cavusgil, Georgia State; Michael Czinkota, Georgetown; and Gary Knight, Willamette University, Editors

- *Creative Solutions to Global Business Negotiations, Second Edition* by Claude Cellich and Jain Subhash
- *Doing Business in Russia: A Concise Guide, Volume I* by Anatoly Zhuplev
- *Doing Business in Russia: A Concise Guide, Volume II* by Anatoly Zhuplev
- *Major Sociocultural Trends Shaping the Contemporary World* by K.H. Yeganeh
- *Globalization Alternatives: Strategies for the New International Economy* by Joseph Mark Munoz
- *Doing Business in the United States: A Guide for Small Business Entrepreneurs with a Global Mindset* by Anatoly Zhuplev, Matthew Stefl, and Andrew Rohm
- *In Search for the Soul of International Business* by Michael R. Czinkota
- *Entering the Chinese e-Merging Market* by Danai Krokou

Announcing the Business Expert Press Digital Library

Concise e-books business students need for classroom and research

This book can also be purchased in an e-book collection by your library as

- a one-time purchase,
- that is owned forever,
- allows for simultaneous readers,
- has no restrictions on printing, and
- can be downloaded as PDFs from within the library community.

Our digital library collections are a great solution to beat the rising cost of textbooks. E-books can be loaded into their course management systems or onto student's e-book readers.
The **Business Expert Press** digital libraries are very affordable, with no obligation to buy in future years. For more information, please visit **www.businessexpertpress.com/librarians**. To set up a trial in the United States, please email **sales@businessexpertpress.com.**

CPSIA information can be obtained
at www.ICGtesting.com
Printed in the USA
LVHW020456260419
615650LV00002B/3/P

9 781948 198844